Table of Contents

The E-M5 Mark III Menu System Simplified
by David Thorpe
Content © David Thorpe.
All Rights Reserved
Published in the United Kingdom.
First Publishing Date February
...........February 2020...............

The Controls................................14
    Top Panel............................15
    Rear Panel...........................28
    AutoFocus............................32
Shooting Menu 1......................40
    Reset/Custom Modes.............40
    Picture Mode........................42
    Quality..................................45
    Image Aspect........................48
    Digital Tele-converter............49
    Sequence/Timer etc...............50
Shooting Menu 2......................56
    Bracketing............................56
    HDR.......................................63

Multiple Exposure.................66
Keystone Comp.....................68
Anti-Shock/Silent.................70
High Res Shot......................73
RC Mode..............................74
Video Menu............................76
Movie Mode Settings.............76
Specification Settings............77
AF/IS Settings......................81
Button/Dial/Lever.................86
Display Settings....................88
Sound.................................93
HDMI Output.......................94
Playback Menu.........................95
(Rotation)............................95
Edit....................................95
Print Order..........................98
Reset Protect.......................99
Reset Share Order.................99
Device Connection................99
Custom A1.............................101
AF Mode............................101
AEL/AFL............................108
AF Scanner..........................112

    C-AF Sensitivity...................113
    C-AF Center Start................115
    C-AF Center Priority...........116
Custom A2..............................118
    Mode Settings......................118
    AF Area Pointer...................118
    AF Targeting Pad.................119
    Set Home..............................120
    Custom Settings...................120
Custom A3..............................122
    AF Limiter............................122
    AF Illuminator.....................122
    Face Priority.......................123
    AF Focus Adj.......................124
Custom A4..............................126
    Preset MF Distance..............126
    MF Assist..............................126
    MF Clutch.............................128
    Focus Ring...........................128
    Bulb/Time Focusing............129
    Reset Lens............................129
Custom B.................................130
    Button Function...................130
    Rec Playback.......................132

- Dial Function......................132
- Dial Direction.....................133
- Fn Lever Function...............133
- Fn Lever/Power Lever.........134
- Elec. Zoom Speed................136
- Custom C1..............................137
  - S-AF Release Priority..........137
  - C-AF Release Priority.........138
  - Sequence L Set....................138
  - Sequence H Set....................140
  - Flicker Reduction................140
- Custom C2..............................142
  - Image Stabilizer...................142
  - Image Stabilizer..................144
  - Half Way Release With IS...145
  - Lens I.S. Priority..................147
- Custom D1..............................148
  - Control Settings...................148
  - Info Settings........................150
  - Picture Mode Settings..........154
  - Sequence/Timer...................155
  - Multi Function Settings.......155
- Custom D2..............................157
  - Live View Boost..................157

- Art LV Mode........................158
- LV Close Up Settings..........159
  - Playback Mag.....................162
- PreviewSettings...................162
- Custom D3..............................164
  - Grid Settings.......................164
  - Peaking Settings..................165
  - Histogram Settings..............166
  - Mode Guide........................168
  - Selfie Assist........................168
- Custom D4..............................170
  - Sound..................................170
  - HDMI..................................170
  - USB Mode..........................171
- Custom E1..............................173
  - Exposure Shift....................173
  - EV Step...............................173
  - ISO Step..............................174
  - ISO-Auto Set.......................174
  - ISO-Auto.............................175
  - Noise Filter.........................177
  - Noise Reduct.......................178
- Custom E2..............................180
  - Bulb/Time Timer.................180

Bulb/Time Monitor..............180
  Live Bulb............................181
  Live Time............................181
  Composite Settings..............183
  Flicker Scan........................184
Custom E3..............................185
  Metering..............................185
  AEL Metering......................188
  Spot Metering......................189
Custom F.................................190
  X-Sync.................................190
  Slow Limit...........................191
  Flash/Ambient.....................194
  WB..195
Custom G................................197
  Set...197
  Pixel Count..........................201
  Shading Comp.....................201
  WB..202
  All WB..................................205
  Keep Warm Color...............205
  Color Space.........................206
Custom H1..............................209
  File Name............................209

Edit Filename......................209
dpi Settings..........................210
Copyright Settings...............211
Lens Info Settings................211
Custom H2..................................214
Quick Erase..........................214
RAW+JPG Erase.................214
Priority Set..........................214
Custom I....................................215
EVF Auto Switch.................215
EVF Adjust..........................216
EVF Style.............................216
Info Settings........................217
EVF Grid Settings...............218
Half Way Level...................219
S-OVF...................................219
Custom J1..................................221
Pixel Mapping.....................221
Press-And-Hold-Time.........221
Level Adjust........................222
Touchscreen Settings...........222
Menu Recall.........................223
Fisheye Compensation.........223
Custom J2..................................224

Backlit LCD..........................224
Sleep.......................................224
Auto Power Off....................224
Quick Sleep Mode...............225
Certification.........................226
Setup Menu.............................227
Card Setup...........................227
Time......................................228
Language..............................228
Monitor Setting....................228
Rec View..............................228
Wi-Fi/ Bluetooth Settings....229
Firmware..............................232
My Example Menu..................233
Shooting Menu 1.................233
Shooting Menu 2.................233
Video Menu.........................233
Playback Menu....................234
Custom.................................234
A1...234
A2...235
A3...235
A4...235
B..235

C1 236
C2 236
D1 236
D2 237
D3 237
D4 237
E1 238
E2 238
E3 238
F 238
G 239
H1 239
H2 239
I 239
J1 240
J2 240
Setup Menu 240

The E-M5 Mark III Menu System Simplified

by David Thorpe

Content © David Thorpe. All rights reserved

Published in the United Kingdom

First Publishing Date February 2020

You've just bought your first digital camera, just upgraded from a point and shoot or maybe you've just been idly scanning through the menu options on your E-M5 Mark III and thought "I wonder what that does"? The menu system and controls of the E-M5 Mark III are well presented but necessarily complex. With 6 sections containing hundreds of menu items, even the most experienced user will sometimes find themselves scratching their head and wondering what an entry means.

This small book goes through every menu choice and control and explains (a) what it does and (b) why you might want to do it. It may not inspire you in a literary sense but with its help you may find an E-M5 Mark III tailored to your personal taste inspiring to use.

I sometimes give my opinion on the best setting. It is only my opinion from my personal experience. It is best treated it as merely a starting point for building your own experience.

At the end of the book I go though the menu items as I set them. The aim of this is to give you a working setup without having to learn what each item does straight away. As you use the camera with my settings you will find yourself thinking, "that's really annoying. If only I could change that". You most likely can. Find the item in question and change it. You now have a E-M5 Mark III a little more tailored to you than before. The aim, eventually, is to have a photographic tool that is personal to your needs. Actually, using the custom settings, you can have three different E-M5 Mark IIIs at hand.

If your interest is photographing the dim interiors of medieval churches using a tripod you might set your E-M5 Mark III to Aperture priority f8/

ISO 200/ Silent Shutter. But you also like to photograph your son playing football with his school team on Shutter Priority 1/1000th/ ISO 3200. Your stand camera and your action camera are but a a moment away using the Mode Dial and/or Menu.

It is that flexibility that makes these gems of 21st century technology so functional. It is the same flexibility of setup that can make them seem more the province of the rocket scientist than the artist at times.

The E-M5 Mark III is a small camera in the hand but a big one at heart, giving away nothing in functionality and real world image quality to its bulky full frame competitors.

Time spent learning what the Olympus E-M5 Mark III can do and how to do it will be rewarded by better results. Enjoy!

(Errors or comments contact me at books@dthorpe.net)

The Controls

The majority of control over a complex, dedicated imaging computer, which is what the E-M5 Mark III really is, is via the **Menu(Fig 01)** button. There are a few things so basic that they must be controlled by exterior levers and buttons. Those controls do not differ greatly from the ones which film camera users from the previous century would have been familiar. Set the camera to **M** on the mode dial and you can control shutter speed and aperture directly. Press the **ISO button (Fig 02)** and you have changed the 'film' speed. The rest of the external controls are essentially shortcuts to often used menu items. Here is a brief rundown on the basics of the body controls of the E-M5 Mark III . Refer to the key numbers below for an explanation of their function.**Note:** many of these controls can have their default actions changed to something you find more useful To see the possibilities, go to the menu at **Custom→B.**

Top Panel

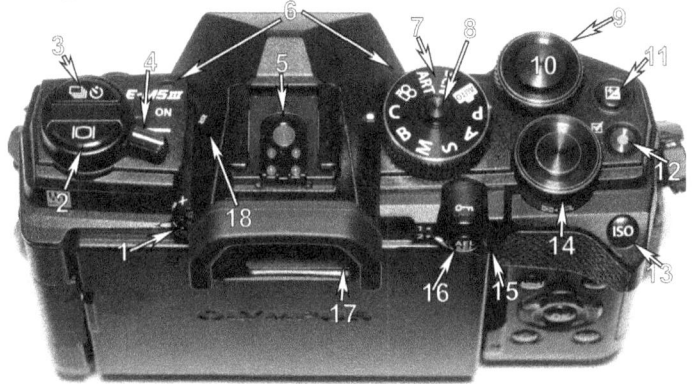

•1 The **Viewfinder dioptre adjustment**. Set it for maximum sharpness when looking at the in-viewfinder information or a detailed image such as a newspaper page

•2 The **LV** button cycles between 3 selections, monitor on, eye level off/ monitor off, eye level on/ or auto switching between them. The obvious setting is auto but under some circumstances, when using a tripod and viewing on the monitor for example, your arm passing near the LV sensor (17) can cause it to switch to the eye level finder. Plus, if you are using the eye level finder and you take the camera from your eye to view the scene, the sensor will auto switch to the monitor. When you put the camera to your eye again, you must wait a moment for the auto switch to take place. In that time, the bird may have flown! Switching explicitly to the eye level finder prevents that. If you are happy to leave the LV on auto switching, you can reassign its function in **Custom B→Button Function**

•3 The **Sequential shooting/Self-timer** button. This brings up strip of shooting mode settings along the bottom of the display from single shot through Pro Cap to Self Timer. There are rather a lot of settings here and it is unlikely you would use all of them so you can limit the selection to your favourites in **Custom→D1 Note:** if you have **Hi Res Shot** enabled in **Shooting Menu 2** you will see that as one of the available choices.

•4 The **On/Off** switch. Pretty straightforward. **Note:** if you find the switch **On** but the camera is dead, it has probably turned itself off according to the setting in **Custom→J2→Auto Power Off**. Switching **Off** and then **On** brings your E-M5 Mark III back to life

•5 The **Hot Shoe** for mounting a flash gun. Olympus's supplied FL-LM3 flash is small and convenient but obviously lacks power for the meatier tasks. Any more powerful flash from Metz, Panasonic or Olympus (and others) made to the Micro Four Thirds standard will work perfectly in **TTL** mode, removing any need for working out aperture settings and conserving battery power at the same time. **Note:** The FL-LM3 can be used to trigger off-camera flash(es) for wireless operation

• The little holes here are actually the left and right stereo microphones. I have never understood how such tiny microphones can record sound so well. Nonetheless, if the sound is important, if you are shooting a music video for example, a higher spec separate stereo mic will sound better. There is a mic input on the left side of the camera body but no headphone output for monitoring

•7 The **Mode Dial** is the arguably the most important control on the camera. The simplest setting is **Auto**. Set to this, the E-M5 Mark III becomes a point and shoot. You have no control over how it takes the picture which makes it particularly irritating to experienced photographers like me. Because it is nearly always right!**P** is for Program where the camera chooses the shutter speed and aperture. The rear dial alters the shutter speed/aperture combination whilst maintaining the same exposure value in this mode so if the camera has chosen 1/125th at f/8, a turn of the rear dial will give you 1/60th at f/11 or 1/250th at f/5.6. **A** is for Aperture Priority. You set the aperture, the camera varies the shutter speed to suit your setting. Aperture is the deciding factor in how much depth of field you have in your picture. For a portrait, you would probably want any distracting background elements to be blurred, in order to focus attention on your subject. For that you would limit your depth of field (obtain shallow depth of field) by using a wide aperture, that is opening your lens to its maximum f/3.5 or f/2.8, f/2 or f/1.4 if you have it. By stopping down to f/8 or lower you gain wide depth of field so that you can get more of your picture in focus. If you are photographing a field of flowers, you can get flowers from near to far in focus. The downside to a small aperture is that to maintain the correct exposure, the shutter speed must be lower. This can lead to blurring of the image due to the camera moving during the exposure. Or, if there is anything moving in your picture, motion blurring. Which brings us to **S**, Shutter Priority. If you are photographing your children running around, they can move a surprisingly long way in, say 1/60th of a second. With **S** you can set a shutter speed to avoid the picture spoiling motion blur that a slow shutter speed would entail. The downside of a high shutter speed is that the lens aperture must be wider to bring in enough light for correct exposure. That, as I previously said, cuts your depth of field, making your focusing very critical, just what you don't want for a child's unpredictable movement. What the shutter speed gives, the aperture takes away and vice versa. As with politics, exposure is the art of compromise. **M** Manual leaves you to set both shutter speed and aperture. It can't achieve anything that **A** or **S** don't but some people prefer to 'do it all'. Note that in all of the previous, I have not mentioned the effect of the **ISO** setting. If you up the **ISO** setting you can have greater depth of field combined with higher shutter speeds. It looks like a win/ win situation. Unfortunately, as with everyday life, there are very few win/ win scenarios. As you raise the **ISO** setting, you are not increasing the amount of light, you are merely amplifying what you have. And as with a radio with a poor signal, the more you turn it up, the more background noise there is. On an imaging sensor, it manifests itself as a random 'rash' on your picture. This juggling act between shutter speed, aperture and ISO is at the heart of photography - only you can decide where your compromise will be. **Note:** a handy use of **M** is to set the shutter speed and aperture you want and then set the **ISO** to **Auto**. It can't brighten the ambient light, though, so ultimately, handy or not, it is one more compromise. **Note:** for **ISO-Auto** to be available in **M**anual mode, **Custom E1.→ISO-Auto** must be set to **All**. The other settings on the **Mode Dial** are less specific. Movie gives you full control over your **Movie** settings, in contrast to the **Rec** button (**3**) which when pressed starts your video using the settings you have set as your default in the **Movie** menu. **Art** gives you direct access to the **Picture Mode** settings for various artistic effects. **SCN** automatically sets you up for a variety of shooting scenarios from fireworks to panorama. The **C** settings are for quick access to your often used settings. I describe the **Custom** settings in the body of the book but in a nutshell they enable you to set the camera up for 3 different tasks and recall them at will. Set **C1** up for photographing dark interiors of buildings on a tripod and **C2** for 30fps sports coverage and the transition is but a menu click away

•**8** The **Lock** button for the **Mode Dial**
•**9** The **Front Dial** has the same multi-faceted role in the control of the E-M5 Mark III as the **Rear Dial**(14} being used for anything from selecting and altering settings on the **Super Control Panel** (I'll call it **SCP** for brevity from now on) to basics like shutter speed and aperture. It is a fair assumption that if it would feel natural to alter something with the dials, Olympus will have implemented it

•**10** The **Shutter Release** button. No need to emphasise the importance of this! It performs more than one function, though. A half press on it will set the exposure and focus point (the exact action can be set while in **Sequence** and **Pro Capture** mode it will keep the shutter firing at high speed as long as you hold it down

•**11** The **Exposure Compensation** button. The light metering system of the E-M5 Mark III is highly sophisticated and rarely wrong footed but it can happen. Sometimes, for pictorial reasons you want a lighter or darker result than the 'correct' exposure gives. In a snow scene, for example, the camera will tend to underexpose, rendering the snow grey rather than white. Good as it is, no auto exposure system is perfect. A press on this button brings up a +/- scale so that you can set the compensation that you judge necessary. I rarely find the exposure needs tweaking beyond + or - 2/3. One of the greatest assets of the **EVF** is that you can see live the effect of any compensation you make. If you prefer not to see the effect, set **Custom I.→S-OVF On**. This will cripple the EVF to more closely resemble a DSLR finder

•**12** The **Movie** button. Press this at any time and the camera will start shooting a video using the default settings you have made in the **Video** menu

•**13** The **ISO** button. **ISO** is the sensitivity of your camera's sensor to light. If the exposure at the light level in an indoor sports stadium yields an exposure of 125th at f/3.5 (full aperture) with **ISO** set to 200 with your kit lens, that will be fine for a static shot. For an action shot, you'll need a minimum of /500th to stop subject movement. You can't open the lens up any more to let in more light. What you can do is set the **ISO** to 800. That will give you your desired 1/500th at f/3.5. As ever with life there are no free lunches. To raise the sensor's sensitivity to light, it simply amplifies the signal. This amplifies any noise present too, which takes a grainy form of random coloured dots. You have to decide for yourself how much noise you can tolerate in order to get the exposure settings you need. I happily use up to 3200 **ISO** without concern. You can reduce noise in post processing to some extent, at the cost of detail

- **14 The Rear Dial see (9)Front Dial**
- **15** The **Function Lever**. This is a two position lever. It enables you to switch between **AF** modes, change dial functions or set the camera to **Movie**. For all the options, see **Custom→B→Fn Lever Function**

•**16** The **AEL/AFL** button. This can be used to focus, set exposure and/or lock both of them. In **Playback** use it to **Protect** selected images.

•**17** The eye sensor. This is tucked away in the eyepiece of the EVF. When you put your eye to the EVF it blocks light to this sensor causing it to switch off the monitor and transfer the signal to the EVF. If you find the monitor flicking on and off, it will be because your hand or arm is coming close to this sensor and blocking it

•**18** The focal plane mark. The line through the symbol here denotes the exact position of the sensing surface of the image sensor in the camera. If you buy a lens which the spec says focuses down 20cm, it means 20 cm from this mark.

Rear Panel

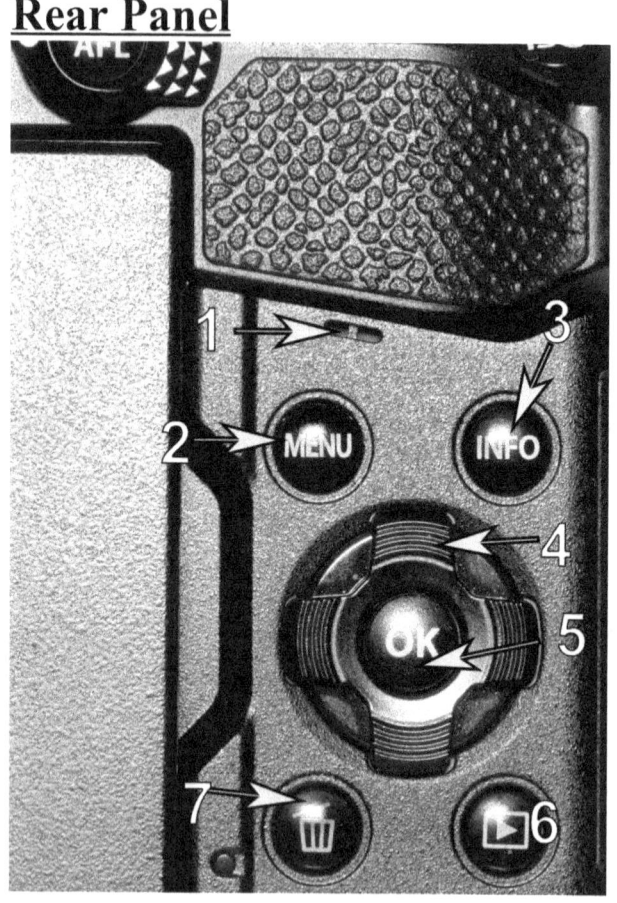

•**1** The **loudspeaker** Studio monitor it isn't but it's good enough to check that sound has been recorded properly
•**2** The **Menu** button. As you'd expect it accesses the menu. It also serves as

an escape button for the menu system, stepping back through buried menu items

•3 The **Info** button. This switches between screens showing image only, shooting information, histogram and level gauge depending on the settings in **Custom→D1**. It performs a similar function in **Playback**. **Note:** If you press and hold the **INFO** button you can scroll through the screens using the front or rear dials

•4 The **Arrow Pad.** It is true it doesn't have arrows but it if you treat each pad logically as left, right, up or down it is an intuitive way of moving the **AF Targets** around the screen or selecting parameters on the **SCP**. In **Custom→B.→▨ Function** you can set the pad to **Direct Function** where you can reprogram the right and down arrows while retaining the focusing functions

•**5** The OK button. Apart from the obvious confirmation of menu items and dialog boxes, this invokes the rather wonderful **SCP** which puts every important shooting control on one quick access screen for viewing and changing if needed. The **SCP** is touch sensitive for quick selection and change of settings and is the most straightforward and efficient way of controlling a complex camera

•**6** The **Playback** button. It accesses the images stored on the camera for review

•**7** The **erase** button. In the unlikely event that anyone takes a less than perfect picture on the E-M5 Mark III, bring it up in **Playback** mode and press this to dispense with the offending image

• there is another **Fn** button on the front of the camera beside the lens and falling comfortably under the ring finger. By default it is set to **Preview** and pushing it stops the camera down to your shooting aperture so that you can see directly the depth of field effect you are getting It can be reprogrammed, of course

• On the left hand side of the camera is a vertical row of sockets. From the top they are the remote microphone input, remote release socket, HDM1 connection and USB socket. This can connect the camera to your computer for downloading images or be used to charge the battery in situ. It cannot power the camera while shooting.

AutoFocus

There are two aspects to the E-M5 Mark III 's autofocus capabilities, the **Target Area** and the **Focus Mode**. I'll deal with the **Target Area** first. In order to do anything, the focusing system must find or be given a target on which to focus. You can leave this to the camera to decide if you wish. Or you can narrow the target field down through a series of configurations until you pinpoint a tiny area yourself. The more you narrow the target area, the easier it is for the camera to know exactly where you wish to focus. As I keep pointing out, though there are no free lunches in photography. The more you narrow the area down, the harder it can become to keep the focus point exactly where you want it, especially with a moving subject. On the other hand, if you leave the camera to choose the target, it may well not match your wishes. Here's a brief run down of the **Target Area** settings.

All The camera chooses the target by dividing the image area into an 11x11 grid and picking the most likely area. In practise, this usually means one of the closer areas. The camera picks well and most of the time its pick will coincide with yours. The beauty of the **All Target Area** is that most of the time the camera will focus on the 'correct' area with no intervention on your part. Where this system falls down is hen the area on which you wish to focus is quite small or similar to the background. The camera in that case may well focus on the background itself. You can lessen the chances of that happening by using one of the other **Target Area**s, for example:

The **5x5** grid which does the same thing as **All** but narrows the area the camera has to scan thus increasing both the accuracy and speed of target acquisition. Speed because the E-M5 Mark III's chip has less analysis to do, accuracy because you have told more closely where to look in the image. This speed and accuracy advantage accrues with smaller grids down to:

5 Target. This cross shape is possibly most useful for moving subjects where you can keep up with the subject's movement. A cyclist or runner, for example. The cross gives you a margin of error for your placing but at the same time is leaves the camera in little doubt about your intended focusing area.

Single. This is most useful for single shot mode. It tells the camera quite exactly where you wish to focus so there is no room for error. It is excellent for moving subjects since it frees all the camera's computing power for tracking and predicting the subject's movement but it can be difficult - or impossible - to keep the box over the subject so the **5 Target** may be more practical. A standard technique for still subjects is to place the focus area where you wish to focus and then half press the shutter release. Keep it half pressed, re-frame the subject and fire. This is generally quicker and much more flexible than moving the focus area around the frame with the arrow keys.

[·]s

Small Target This does the same as **Single** but is even more precise. If you are photographing something through a grill or a bird partially hidden by tree branches, for example, this can be the answer. It's not a good choice for everyday use because many subjects do not have enough detail to enable this method to work. The E-M5 Mark III's focusing system requires some detail with a level of contrast to focus easily. Many objects have areas on them that are plain and if the **Small Target** is pointed at one of those areas, even though the rest of the object has markings, correct focus won't be possible.

Now, the **Focus Mode**s. There are four basic ones, any others being combinations of them.

• **S-AF** The most straightforward mode. Press the shutter button once, the camera focuses and a picture is taken. This takes a lot longer to write than it does to happen. Focusing is, for practical purposes, instantaneous. It works well for slower moving subjects, too. The press shutter button/focus/shoot cycle is so quick that subject movement during the process is negligible and easily covered by the depth of focus.

• **C-AF** For moving subjects. It processes the image information as it comes in and predicts the movement, adjusting focus while the shutter button is half pressed. All you need to do is press the shutter when you see the shot. For sequence shooting **C-AF** is imperative so that the focus remains on the subject and you can pick the best shots from your burst with confidence that will all be sharp. Naturally, you must keep the **Target Area** on your subject. You can use **All** with **C-AF** but while it will work with a well delineated subject it is a lot of computing for the camera to do. The more restricted **Target Area**s are more reliable provided you can keep them on the subject

• **C-AF+(TR)acking** This is similar to **C-AF** except that once focus is locked on to the subject it will keep the focus box on the subject automatically, the focus box showing little 'handles' when it is locked on (and going red when it loses lock). Let's say you are set to the **5 Point Target Area** and have focus on a football player. With **C-AF**, if your **Target Area** strays from the player as he weaves around, focus will go to wherever the focus box is pointed. With **TR**acking, once focus is locked, the box will follow the player around wherever he or she weaves. This sounds the obvious method to use but in practice it depends on the circumstances. If the player is in a melee and other other players are weaving in and out and across your view, the camera will not be able to keep up and you will have no focus at all. If this is happening all the time, it will lose you shots. With standard **C-AF** if the camera loses a clear view you can place the **5 Point** near where the player is and half press the shutter as soon there is a clear view, picking up where you left off. Circumstances and experience will dictates what it best. A great scenario

for **TR**acking is photographing a single player in a band where you are using a wide aperture and have very little depth of field. Lock the focus on them and the E-M5 Mark III will happily track them. Just press the button when the shot occurs.
• **MF** Manual focus. It is not as difficult as it sounds, especially with the **Magnify** and **Peaking** focusing aids. With practice, it is highly flexible since you can focus anywhere on the screen immediately. Imagine you are photographing two children interacting, with only enough depth of field to have one of them critically sharp at a time. Instead of having to set or manipulate a **Target Area** to move the focus point, all you have to do is watch the scene and turn the focusing ring as necessary.

Shooting Menu 1

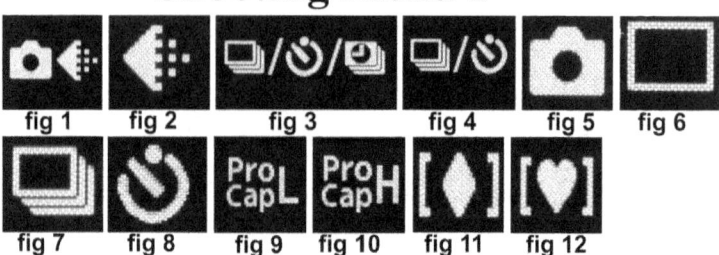

Reset/Custom Modes
Reset
• **Full** Got in a complete muddle with your settings? This **Reset**s the camera to its default settings as it came from the box but does leaves date, time and a few essentials in place

• **Basic** is less and extreme than **Full** and will leave in place your settings for the **Fn** button and **Lever** operations. If you have made a setting that you do not want but cannot recall what it was, it makes sense to try a **Basic** reset first

Assign to Custom Mode
Custom Modes are an important aspect of Olympus digital cameras. You can go through every menu

setting on the camera and set them how you prefer, then assign that combination of settings to a **Custom Mode**. There are three completely independent **C** settings available, Then, whenever you set the camera to that **Custom Mode** it will call up those settings. This includes the lens aperture so if you have the lens set to f/2.8 when you save the **Custom** setting all lenses will open set to f/2/8. If the lens is slower than that, f/4, say, it will open at the widest aperture of the lens fitted. **Note:** If your **C** setting has ISO set to 200 and you alter it while shooting to 1600, when you turn the camera off and on again, it will have reverted to ISO 200. The camera does not reset the **C** mode on going to **Sleep**, though, only on **Power Off**. If under trying photographic conditions, you become confused, having made several alterations to the settings to suit your subject, switching the camera off and back on again will always revert the settings to your known state, a useful fail-safe.

Recall from Custom Mode

Recall one of the three **C** settings for use. I'd suggest setting up a couple of basic settings, **C** for everyday photography, say and **C2** for action/ follow focus work. **Note:** you can recall a saved setting to any exposure mode, Aperture priority, Shutter priority etc but the mode is not changed. That is to say, if you have **C1** set to invoke **A** but you **Recall** it while set to **S** mode, the mode remains **S**. It is best, when you **Recall** a **C**ustom setting that the **Mode Dial** is set to **C/C2/C3** therefore.

Picture Mode

The comprehensive list of **Picture Modes** is self-explanatory. There are some highly sophisticated effects here all of which are shown in real time on the monitor. You can view them in the EVF, too. When choosing an effect, a press on the right cursor button will bring up a selection of parameters which can be altered to taste. Depending on the effect chosen, these will affect sharpness, contrast, brightness and so on. Some effects allow you to add one effect to another or change the nature of the chosen effect. Mono, for example, gives you a choice of colour filter emulations, red to darken the sky for example but also to blue tone the subject and even make it high or low key. I find the best way to try the modes is from the **SCP S**uper **C**ontrol **P**anel. Just highlight **Picture Mode** (top right), press **OK** and a complete list of the modes appears at the bottom of the screen. You can then scroll through them with the effect showing on screen.**Note:** there are many choices here including some you will never use. You can narrow down the modes displayed by ticking or

unticking items in **Custom Menu→D1.→Picture Mode Settings**.
(fig 1)
Note: This menu item enables you to set the quality of still images you want to shoot. The **JPG** settings displayed here are governed by your choices in **Custom Menu G→**(fig 2) **Set**

• **RAW** files consist of the digital data information straight off the sensor with no processing done other than the very basics. This leaves it to you to make the best use of the image data in post processing. **RAW** files are a little like a negative in film photography. All the image information is there but a print must be made in order to conveniently display the image

• **JPG** is more like a print. The EM-5 MkIII takes the image information from the sensor and processes it into conveniently small files in a globally

viewable form. The downside of **JPG** is that in compressing and processing the image, information is irretrievably lost and at high compression rates like **Basic** unpleasant artifacts may be introduced. This will matter for some uses and not to others. However, the E-M5 MkIII offers the best of both worlds since it can make both **RAW** and **JPG** files simultaneously each time you press the shutter. Thus, if you want to quickly send some pictures off to a social networking site you have the **JPG** to hand while if you wish later to make a print for framing from the same image you have the **RAW** file to work with. Personally I only shoot in **RAW** or **Large JPG** simply because it is so easy to resize down in camera or post processing while keeping the original
• **Size** choices are **Large**/ **Medium**/ **Small** for physical picture size and for **JPG** quality choices Super Fine - Fine

- **Normal** - **B**asic. To give an example of the range available, an example shot I took at **LSF** comes in at 11.9MB. The same shot at **SB** is just 363Kb! **Notes:RAW** files are always at the maximum pixel count for the **Image Aspect** chosen. Large files are always at the maximum pixel count for the **Image Aspect** chosen. It would be impractical to show every combination of file size and quality available in this menu, so the choice of **JPG**s is limited to four. If you go to the top menu item (**Set**) in the **G** section of the **Custom** menu you can select which choices show in the **Still Image Quality** list. There's more! If you go to the menu item **Pixel Count** in the same menu you can choose the pixel dimensions the camera should use for **M**iddle and **S**mall. To recap, the **JPG** image quality in which you wish to shoot is set with this menu item. The choices it offers are set in **G** section of the **Custom** menu. **Note:** If you shoot high speed sequences, using **RAW** or **RAW+JPG**, the camera will shoot fewer images before slowing down and will take longer to write them to the SD Card(s). For most purposes this won't really hamper you because the camera has plenty of processing power and a large buffer to store images until they are written. It is more a factor if you want to shoot long sequence with only short intervals between them

Image Aspect

• **4:3** the native size of the sensor and therefore the highest pixel count
• **16:9** the de facto standard for digital video
• **3:2** the standard for full frame and APS-C cameras and therefore familiar to those who have previously owned such a camera. It has no particular merit in an artistic sense and became standard only because the originator of

the 35mm format needed to use 16mm film stock and this was a logical aspect to make the best of it

• **1:1** the square format as was used by 6x6cm film cameras

• **3:4** saves you turning the camera to portrait orientation for upright 4:3 shots at the cost of image resolution. Test how lazy you are here!

Note: there is a helpful list of all the resolutions possible with each ratio, including **High Res** shown as you run through the options.

Digital Tele-converter

This works by cropping the sensor to 2592x1944 px and then sampling it back up to 5184x3888 px, giving the effect of doubling the focal length of the lens. In doing this sharpness is lost, naturally, since you are using only a cropped central portion of the sensor for your image. Keep in mind that if your usage for the picture is is below 2592 pixels wide, a high quality print of 10 inches across, say, or viewing on a 1920x1080 monitor you would be better simply to crop the image in post processing since there is no need to upsample. In these days of cheap and sharp zoom lenses there is little need for a digital zoom. The **Digital Tele Converter** can be used in video but again I find the effect distinctly inferior to using a zoom to enlarge the image. One for emergencies only!

(fig 3)
(fig 4)

 The long list of options here can seem overwhelming. Once you understand what each option is, you might want to go to **Custom → D1→(fig 5) Settings** where you can select which choices are listed. It is unlikely you will use them all.

- **(fig 6)** denotes single shot mode. One press on the shutter results in one frame exposed
- **(fig 7)** denotes a sequence mode. Press and hold the shutter button down and the camera continues to shoot until (a)it is released (b) it has shot the preset number of frames you set or (c) the buffer runs out and the camera stops shooting while images are saved to the SD card
- **(fig 8)** denotes a delayed action
- **(fig 9, 10)** Pro Capture, a high speed capture mode up to 30fps

  There are 3 types of shutter available.
- **(fig 6)** a plain rectangle means the mechanical shutter
- **(fig 11)** a diamond icon denotes Anti-Shock, a hybrid mechanical/electronic arrangement, electronic first shutter blind, mechanical second blind. This eliminates any possibility of 'shutter shock', a slight double

imaging which can be caused by the force of the shutter blind coming to its end stop

- **(fig 12)** the heart icon denotes a fully electronic shutter, no parts move

I'll give a brief explanation of why you have the 3 shutter types. The shutter used on advanced cameras is called a focal plane shutter. It consists of two metal curtains which are moved at high speed across the sensor to give you your chosen exposure time. When the first curtain hits the side frame of the sensor at the end of its rapid travel, it has a tendency to jolt the camera. That jolt, slight as it is, can cause a double imaging effect known as shutter shock. It will only be seen at high image magnifications and shows itself as blurring of the image. It occurs between shutter speeds from roughly 1/60th to 1/320th. Careful shutter design has reduced the effect to the point where on the E-M5 Mark III it will rarely, if ever be noticed. However, the effect can be completely eliminated by using not the mechanical shutter but an electronic one, represented by a heart icon. The electronic shutter has no moving parts hence no shutter shock. Unfortunately, because of the way it functions, the electronic shutter can lead to a slight distortion of a moving subject. Which is why the hybrid shutter, denoted by a diamond icon exists. It uses the electronic shutter for the first curtain and the mechanical one for the second curtain over the range of potential shock speeds, thus avoiding both shutter shock and image distortion. **Note:** Which shutter to use? The electronic one if you want silent operation and the highest shutter (1/32,000th) and sequence speeds. The mechanical one for the highest flash sync speeds (1/250th, as opposed to the 1/50th of the **Silent Shutter**). The hybrid one is probably generally best although it limits the fastest shutter speed to the same 1/8000th as the mechanical shutter with flash the same at 1/250th. With the electronic silent shutter, flash sync speed is limited to 1/45th and must be activated in **Shooting Menu 2→Anti-Shock/Silent→Silent Mode Settings**

Intrvl.Sh./Time Lapse

This is for those highly speeded up time effects you see so often on TV. **Note:** it makes sense to use the **Silent Shutter** for this to save unnecessary wear and tear on the mechanical shutter and to conserve battery power.

Number of Frames

Set up to 999.

Start Waiting Time

If you want to start shooting at 6am, you can set this to 12 hours the evening before to save getting up.

Interval Length

The time between each shot.

Time Lapse Movie

You can have the camera make your time lapse sequence into a movie automatically using the parameters set bepow. It will retain the individual stills.

Movie Settings

Set the resolution and frame rate of your movie here. The FHD and 4K settings do not include 25 or 30fps, maxing at 15 and 5 frames p[er second respectively. This can look a little jerky but most imaging software will allow you to assemble the frames into faster rates if you need.

Shooting Menu 2

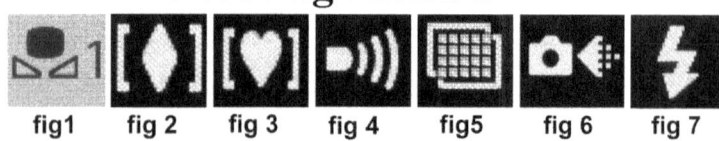

fig1　　fig 2　　fig 3　　fig 4　　fig5　　fig 6　　fig 7

Bracketing

Under some circumstances it is hard to know if the camera will be able to automatically cope or whether, if it does, it will give the result you want. Let's say you are shooting a street scene with people walking towards you with the sun behind them, shining onto their backs, what is known as contre-jour lighting. Will the picture look best with a halo effect around the people. Or do you need detail in their faces? If you set AE (Automatic Exposure) bracketing to On, 5f, 1.0EV, for example, when you press the shutter it will make an exposure at the normal setting, then 2 stops below normal, 1stop below, 1 stop above and finally 2 stops above. One of those frames should match what you wanted to see. The E-M5 Mark III allows you to bracket several useful parameters. **Note:** you can bracket parameters concurrently, **ISO** with **AE**, for example but you can end up with an awful lot of files since if you bracket two parameters at 5 steps, you end up with 11 images, one with all parameters standard and the others altered as you set. It does not give you **ISO** and **AE** altered on one image.

AE BKT

 Brackets the exposure settings (as outlined above). Note that if you set the camera to **Sequential** Shooting the number of frames set for **Bracketing** will fire off and stop. This is a lot more convenient than pressing the shutter time after time. I find 3 frames, 1 stop over and 1 stop under about right. It would be very rare for the E-M5 Mark III to get the exposure more than a stop out.

WB BKT

Brackets the **White Balance**, altering the colour in separately selectable steps. There is no point in using this if shooting **RAW** files as you can alter the **White Balance** as you wish after shooting. **A-B** means Amber to Blue and **G-M** Green to Magenta. If you use this, you will use a lot of card storage space, as for each of the frames shot you are making up to 6 different versions. It's almost impossible to understand the effect of this complex setting. The best way to get to grips with it would be to wait until you found you had a regular problem with the white balance on a particular type of subject (under fluorescent light, say) and play with this until it gives you a range of results that you prefer. This bracketing procedure seems a little haphazard to me and I would recommend setting white balance manually from a sheet of white paper using one of the **Capture WB** and **Info** Settings (Fig 1) on the **SCP** in preference. **Note:** if you find you cannot alter **WB** at any time, check that you do not have an **Art Filter** selected as some of these use it as part of the filter.

FL BKT

(Flash Bracket) Shoots 3 frames at different flash levels, one each time the shutter is pressed or 3 in a row if you have sequence set. If you do have sequence set, the camera will only fire off a frame when the flash is ready to give the necessary power. This function is particularly useful under tricky conditions or with very dark or light subjects where results can be unpredictable. Don't expect a long battery life if you use **FL BKT** a lot!

ISO BKT

This sets the camera to shoot 3 frames, altering the **ISO** for two of them. Let's say you are shooting Aperture Priority, f/4 and the camera has set a shutter speed of 1/500th. If you have set **ISO** to 400, the first frame will be at ISO400, the next at 200 and the next at 800 (assuming you have set the modification amount to 1.0 EV). It has much the same effect as **AE BKT** in that it shoots one darker and one lighter frame but unlike AE BKT neither aperture nor shutter speed change. You can set the modification to -+0.3, -+0.7 or -+1.0 EV. Given how much you can tweak the images from the E-M5 Mark III's sensor in post processing, -+1.0 EV makes the most sense

Art BKT

Set to **On** you can select any number of the **Art Filters** such as **Pop Art** or **Pin Hole** and the camera will shoot your picture in sequence with the Art Filters you have selected one after another. As with all these **BKT** settings, if you set the camera to **L** or **H** sequence, it will fire the shutter as many times as necessary. If you set many of the **Art Filters** it may take the camera some time to complete your sequence since they are processor intensive.

Focus BKT

Note: Focus Bracketing works with all lenses, **Stacking** only with the Pro series lenses There are two aspects to focus bracketing, the bracketing itself and the clever focus stacking. Bracketing simply takes a series of frames automatically adjusting the focus point from near to far. Stacking takes focus bracketed frames and combines them in camera into one frame (while retaining the component frames). The main use of this is for macro work where because you are working so close to an object the available depth of field, the amount in focus, will not cover it. The E-M5 Mark III will fire off 8 frames and automatically combine them for often stunning results. You can obtain more depth of field by stopping the lens down, of course but for inescapable optical reasons stopping a Micro Four Thirds lens down beyond f/8 leads to a degradation in sharpness. While **Bracketing** can be done hand held, **Stacking** requires a tripod for technically sound results. **Set Number Of Shots** tells the camera how many frames to take in total. **Set Focus Differential** tells the camera how closely spaced the focusing distance intervals will be. Micro Four Thirds cameras by their nature have more depth of field than larger sensor cameras so to keep the **Bracketing** output to reasonable numbers, I'd suggest 10 shots with a focus differential of 5. **Charge Time** applies if you are shooting with a non-Micro Four Thirds native flash. This just sets a time interval between the shots to give the flash time to recharge. With Micro Four Thirds native equipment, the camera will fire as soon as the flash is ready without manual intervention.

HDR

if you take a picture of scene with an extreme tonal range, the camera's sensor cannot encompass them all. An example would be a picture of a room interior with a small window with a view out onto a garden. A good indoor exposure for the room, the furniture, paintings on the wall etc might be ISO 200 1/25th at f/4. The garden outside might require ISO 200 1/4000th at f/4. A room exposure renders the window a white detail-less rectangle. An exposure for the garden outside renders the interior an inky black. A compromise exposure of 1/250th at f/4 renders nothing satisfactorily. **HDR** takes a series of exposures and combines them, attempting to show detail both in the room and outside the window. The E-M5 Mark III has a long list of **HDR** settings but the first two **HDR1** and **HDR2** are particularly valuable since they automate what can be a complicated process manually. The other options are worth trying in the unlikely event that the first two do not produce a satisfactory image. **HDR1** and **HDR2** take several images and combine them, leaving you with the one **HDR** JPG. The other settings leave you with a series of images to load into your photo software and process there. **Note:** you need not hold down the shutter button while the camera takes the series of frames. Press once and it will continue until finished. If you have the camera set to **RAW** when you shoot an **HDR** image, it will produce an **HDR** JPG plus a normal **RAW** file. **RAW** cannot be processed because if it was, it would no longer be **RAW**. If you ever shoot a **RAW** image and wish you had shot it in **HDR** but didn't, you could try opening it in Lightroom or Photoshop, alter the exposure -1 or -2 stops and save it as a separate image. Then alter the exposure +1 or +2 and save that. You now have 3 images, one as shot, one dark and one light. You can now combine those to make an **HDR** image. Better to do it when taken but worth a try if you didn't.

HDR1

Attempts to make a normal looking image

HDR2

Renders a more processed looking image.

Multiple Exposure

This enables you to shoot several images onto one frame and combine them. If this is greyed out, check on the **SCP** you are using an appropriate **Picture Mode** since some are not compatible with this setting. If **Multiple Exposure** is active you will see an icon showing two overlapping rectangles on the top centre of the screen.

Number of Frames

Set to **2f**, take a picture and the image remains on screen. Reframe as desired and when you press the shutter again, this shot is combined with the first shot and saved as one frame. The individual frames are lost. This will tend to give very light images since the original exposures are added to each other. Which is why you would normally set this next item -

Auto Gain

On.

Overlay

This is greyed out unless you have a **RAW** image on the card to form the basis of the **Multiple Exposure** and **Auto Gain** is set **On**. When you set **Overlay** to **On** you are shown thumbnails of the viable images. Select the image you wish to use as the basis of your overlay and your next frame will be overlaid on that. You are left with 2 images on the card, your original frame and that frame combined with the last one. If you wish to combine more than 2 frames, select the combined frame and the next frame you shoot will be added to that. Unless you have a definite idea in mind, more than 2 frames overlaid tend to simply look confusing. Note that you can manipulate your overlays further in the **Playback** Menu by pressing the Menu button and selecting Edit. This will enable you to select two or more of your images for the camera to merge. You can also alter the relative density of the images but even given the clarity of the camera screen, this is a little tortuous and more easily done in post processing.

Keystone Comp.

This only operates in **P**, **A**, **S** and **M** modes. It is best done with the camera on a tripod. It enables you to correct or if you wish exaggerate perspective effects via the front and rear dials. If you are shooting a room with a wide angle lens and need to tilt the camera you will see how out of kilter the verticals become. It can look quite ugly. **Keystone Comp.** brings your image more into line with what your eye sees. This used to be done with (very expensive) tilting lenses. Because of the way it works, this facility crops your picture. Use the arrow keys to select the area of the crop you wish to use. Keystone Comp. doesn't do anything than cannot be done in post processing but it can be valuable to correct 'on the job', as it were. This is something that could have been a gimmick but Olympus's implementation of it, like their **HDR** is genuinely useful. While **Keystone Comp** is activated,the front and rear dials are used to control it. If you wish to change exposure settings, press the **Info** button. **Note:** that with **Keystone Comp.** on many of the camera's other facilities and modes, for example **Sequence**

Shooting and **Live Time** are disabled so don't switch it on unless you are using it. And if you can't set access something, check that this is **Off** as a first port of call. It is greyed out if bracketing (**BKT**) is enabled.

Anti-Shock(fig 2)/Silent(fig 3)

Anti-Shock(fig 3)

All focal plane shutters are prone to a phenomenon called shutter shock. It is caused by the rapid deceleration of the first curtain of the shutter as it reaches the frame edge. It is a very mild effect mainly seen at high magnifications and using shutter speeds between about 1/60th and 1/320th. Under most circumstances it is unnoticeable. It can be eliminated by the use of an electronic first curtain which is what switching on **Anti-Shock** does. For general use, set the delay time to 0, of course. Unless you have reason not to, this is likely to be your most useful all round setting.

Silent (fig 3)

The **Silent** shutter is very useful under circumstances where normal camera noise would be intrusive. Being fully electronic, the Silent shutter, denoted always by a heart shaped icon, cannot suffer from shutter shock. Its disadvantages are a small distortion when used with fast moving objects and flash synchronization is limited to 1/45th which may be a problem for fill-in flash on a bright day. In general, you will want a higher shutter speed than 1/45th with flash so use **Anti-Shock** or the normal fully mechanical mode.

Noise reduction

When very long (great than 1s) exposure times are used, all image sensors generates random noise in the form of bright coloured pixels.

With **Noise ReductionOn** the camera will seek out and eliminate those pixels. To do this takes the same amount of time as making the exposure. Thus a 30s exposure will take 30s to clean up, giving a minimum time between shots of 1m. You may prefer a slightly flawed image to the possibility of missing a shot while you are waiting.**Note:** a major problem with this setting is that when **On** you will hear a 'clunk' shutter sound which nullifies the silence of the shutter.

Silent (fig 3) Mode Settings

• **(fig 4)** Suppress or allow confirmatory beeps, such as when focus is acquired

• **AF Illuminator** In dark conditions the camera will emit a discreet pulse of light to enable the autofocus to lock on quickly. This obviously compromises the 'stealth' uses of the **Silent Shutter**. In all but the dimmest

conditions autofocus will work without **AF Illuminator** but may be slower and subject to 'hunting'
• **Flash Mode** Using the flash in **Silent Mode** obviously compromises any 'stealth' use so you can disable it

High Res Shot

This enables the E-M5 Mark III to 'shoot above its weight'! Where the standard picture dimensions in 4:3 aspect ratio are 5184x3888, with the 25Mp **Hi-Res** this is increased to 5760x4320 and with 50Mp to 8160x6120 pixels. 50mp Hi-Res actually approaches the maximum many lenses can resolve! Once you have selected this mode (fig 5), you can choose which flavour you require by going to **Shooting Menu 1**→(fig 6) **Note:** taking a picture in **Hi-Res** mode is not instantaneous. The camera takes a picture then shifts the sensor and merges the results to make the final image. This takes several seconds so the camera is best used on a tripod. With a subject like a landscape, for example some movement of leaves on trees can be tolerated but for product photography the camera must be held solid. It is also best to use a delay to allow the camera to settle down from the shutter push. 50Mp is very intolerant of any technical laxness.

(fig 7)Charge Time

If using a Micro Four Thirds standard flash the camera can ask the flash when it is ready to fire. If not, you can set a delay here long enough for it to recharge.

(fig 7)RC Mode

With this on the camera can control up to three flashes for **R**emote **C**ontrol. Attach the supplied Olympus flash and it will operate them without trouble provided they are all set to the same **Group** and

Channel. I can't be more specific here because different flashes will require different settings on the flashes themselves. For remotely using one flash, just set **RC On**, the remote flash to TTL and both to the same Channel it will expose correctly when triggered from the Olympus flash.

Video Menu

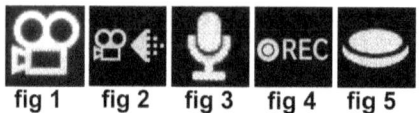

fig 1　fig 2　fig 3　fig 4　fig 5

Movie (fig 1)Mode Settings

Although you can use **P** and **A** modes for video it is best not to, since they take control of the shutter speed. For natural looking movement in video it is best to use a shutter speed of twice the frame rate, so for 25fps, use 1/50th and for 60fps use 1/120th. Both **S**hutter priority and **M** let you choose the shutter speed. If you want automatic exposure, therefore, use **S** and let the camera take care of the aperture. Experienced videographers often prefer **M** to avoid the momentary darkening and lightening of the shots as the camera alters the aperture in changing light. The eye is much more tolerant of dark or light video than it is of under or over exposed stills. Because of the low shutter speeds used for video, neutral density filters are useful to avoid shooting at f/16 or f/22 with consequent diffraction effects and loss of sharpness. ND filters also allow you to open the aperture for shallow depth of field.

Flicker Scan

Under artificial lighting it is possible that you will see a banding/flickering effect on the screen. Set this on and then turn the front or rear dials. This will subtly change the shutter speed so as to nullify the effect.

(fig 1)Specification Settings
(fig 2)

This is where you set your choice of quality for your videos. The camera offers everything from 24 to 60 frames per second and 120fps slow motion. Video is recorded in the **MOV** format which, although orginally an Apple format, is compatible with all software and hardware these days. There's a choice of compression rates plus **HD** (1280x720), **FHD** (1920x1080),**4K** (3840x2160) and **C4K** (4096x2160).**HD** is becoming a little passé these days and most video is shot **FHD**. However, **4K** is gaining ground and even if you do not have a **4K** TV to watch your videos, it has advantages in video editing. Down-sampling to **FHD** lowers noise, for example. If you are shooting to finally output **FHD** video, by shooting in **4K** initially you have the flexibility to crop, zoom and pan around your image in your existing software. As a rule of thumb, for any given **Size** and **fps**, the higher the **Bit Rate** the better the quality. The top rate is **A-I,** **A**ll-**I**ntra, with **N**ormal, **F**ine and **S**uper **F**ine being the other choices. **Note:** the difference between **4K** and **C4K** is that **C4K** is primarily intended for cinema use. For that reason it can only be used at the cinema frame rate of 24fps. If converted to the standard video aspect ratio of **16:9** it will either show black bars at each end of the picture or be cropped slightly. This is because the aspect ratio of **C4K** is **1.9:1**. For most video intended for YouTube or watching on your TV, **4K** is a better choice, being simply twice the width and height of **FHD**. (**4K** TV is 3840x2160 pixels).

• **25 or 30fps?** As a rule of thumb, if you live in North America you will use 30fps, in Europe 25fps. There are two worldwide standards for TV transmission, **PAL**, 25fps and **NTSC**, 30fps. In reality, modern equipment happily adjusts to whatever frame rate you feed it, as does YouTube and all the social media sites you may wish to post video

- **50 or 60fps?** You'd use these frame rates for faster moving subjects for smoother depiction of movement. They are best avoided unless you know what you are doing since some software may misinterpret and give you half speed motion. They also double the data and storage required

(fig 1)Noise Filter

If you are using high ISO settings you may find the noise level on your video unacceptable. You can suppress noise at 3 levels or not at all here. Noise reduction comes at the expense of image detail so which setting you use depends on your own tolerance of image noise levels. For myself, I will accept quite a high level of noise in order to retain detail since I think it looks more realistic so I turn this off. It's personal, though, and for everyday use Olympus's **Standard** setting is a sensible compromise.

(fig 1)Picture Mode

This is one I find hard counter-intuitive to say the least! If you have a **Picture Mode** set in **Shooting Menu 1**, with this set to **Off**, your video will be shot in that setting. So, if you set **Picture Mode→Monochrome**, your video will be shot in monochrome. Set this to **On** and the **Picture Mode** is disabled and your video will be shot in a standard, flat setting suitable for editing. This seems counter-intuitive to me but I think Olympus see it as **On** means you have an editable video where with it **Off** your video is stuck with the **Picture Mode** setting which cannot, obviously, be edited away.

(fig 1)AF/IS Settings

There are two ways to start a video, you can use the **Shutter button** or the **Rec button**. The choice for this is under **Shutter Function** in

Button/Dial/Lever in this **Video Menu**. If **Shutter Function** is set to (fig 4) then when the **Mode** dial is set to Movie, video recording is started and stopped with the **Rec Button**. If set to (fig 5) start and stop is via the **Shutter button**. Note: **S-AF** and **S-AF+MF** only work if **Shutter Function** is set to (fig 4).

AF Mode

• **S-AF**(single autofocus) - Half press the shutter button to focus then press the **Rec Button** to start and stop video recording. A half press of the shutter button while shooting will re-focus. This isn't ideal because the focusing is very sudden which looks awful in video. Best used on subjects where, once focused they will not move very much

• **C-AF** (continuous autofocus) - the camera will focus automatically all the time. If the camera mis-focuses, a half press on the shutter button at any time will shift focus to your chosen point

• **MF** (manual focus) - is the professional's choice because you can control the exact speed of focus and the exact focusing point. **Focus Peaking** is an enormous help here. **MF** is very difficult on moving subjects

• **S-AF+MF** - allows you to modify the camera's focus point by making the lens focusing ring active so that you can override the camera at any time. Handy for situations where you have limited depth of field and the camera focus spot is not precise enough

• **C-AF+TR** (tracking) - allows you to pick a focus point which the camera will track and attempt to keep in focus. A half press on the shutter button brings up a green box. Line this up with whatever you want to keep in focus and start the video with whichever button you have set to do so

• **Preset MF** - this is good for what is known as pulling focus (it is also a bit tricky to operate). Let's say you want to open your shot focused on a bush in a garden and finish it focused on the house behind. First of all, set a **Fn** button to **Preset MF Distance** in **Button/Dial/Lever** in this **Video Menu**. Now, set the focus mode to **Preset MF**. Press **Menu** twice to take you back to the monitor. Press **OK**. A Preset MF box comes up. Press **Info** and turn the focus ring until you have focus on the house. Press **OK**. Now set the focus mode to **S-AF** and focus on the bush. Start the video. When you are ready, press the **Fn** button previously set and focus will shift to your preset, the house. The focus shift will be fairly slow as is best for video. **Note:** If you are using an Olympus lens with the focusing ring clutch you can preset a distance more easily. Pull the clutch back and set focus. Push it forward and and the lens will autofocus again. At any time, however, you can pull back the focus clutch and the focus distance will be where you previously set it. This focus change is a little abrupt for video. It can be used for effect but is probably better used when shooting stills

(fig 1)Image Stabilizer

Use **Off** when the camera is on a tripod or otherwise securely held steady. **M-IS 1** uses the superb sensor stabilization combined with digital stabilization. This crops the image a little and given the efficiency of the sensor stabilization alone is rarely necessary. **M-IS 2** is the sensor stabilization alone and as ever with Olympus, vies with very best on any camera system.

(fig 1)Button/Dial/Lever
(fig 1)Button Function

These are all straightforward and the defaults are well chosen. When Olympus mark a button it is always something crucial like **ISO** and something which will require instant access. **These Button Function**s apply specifically to when **Movie** mode is set. **L-Fn** is the function button on some Olympus lens bodies, notably the Pro series. The **Arrow Pad** Function by default accesses the AF focusing points and positions but can also be set to **Direct Function** which usefully allows the right and down arrows to be re-assigned while the left and up arrows still access the AF focusing functions.

(fig 1)Dial function

You can set the function of the front and rear dials for each shooting mode. Not only that but if you set **Fn Lever Function** to **Mode 1**, the lever will change the function. Hit the **Info** button while viewing the **Dial Function**s to choose the options for the second position.

(fig 1)Fn Lever Function

This determines whether the lever changes the **Dial Function**s (as set above) or **AF** settings. If you choose **Mode 2**, a press on the right arrow key will give you the choice of which parameters it will change. To set it up, set the **AF** parameters selected with the lever in position 1. Now set the lever to position 2 and set what you wish. From then on, the lever toggle between those settings.

(fig 1)Shutter Function
This allows you to use the main shutter button to start/stop video recording while in **Movie** mode. It disables the **Rec** button at the same time. It doesn't affect the stills modes, so while shooting stills you can press the **Rec** button and it will start shooting a video, as before,
(fig 1)Elec.Zoom Speed
 If you have a power zoom lens like the Olympus 12-50mm f/3.5-6.3, this sets the speed with which it will zoom. Since you can control the zoom speed from the zoom ring on the lens, this doesn't have much effect, really.

(fig 1)Display Settings
(fig 1)Control Settings
This sets what happens when you press the **OK** button. With no boxes ticked, it brings up a screen with info on it. You cannot alter any settings

on this screen, it is for information only. A half touch on the shutter button returns you to a clean screen. With **Live Control** ticked, press **OK** and the right and bottom area of the screen show a comprehensive selection of shooting parameters which can be navigated and altered using the front and rear dials and the arrow cursors. With just **Live SCP** ticked, the monitor is covered with the usual **SCP** screen and you can change relevant video parameters. The **SCP** is dismissed with a half press of the shutter button. With both boxes ticked you get just the **SCP**. The obvious choice here is just the **Live Control** because it allows you a clear view of the scene while you are changing settings, unlike **SCP**.

(fig 1)Info Settings

With both boxes unticked the **Info** button does nothing when pressed. **Custom 1** and **Custom 2** give you two screens, each of which you can customise to give the information you wish to see. If you have too much information on a screen it can become confusing so you can set different parameters on the two screens and step through them and the pressing **Info**.

Time Code Settings

• **Time Code Mode** This is of relevance to **NTSC** 30/60fps video makers only. For reasons to do with TV broadcast the 30fps nominal frame rate of **NTSC** is actually 29.97 fps. It is a small difference but because the **Time Code** keeps time by frames shot it leads to inaccuracy when compared to a clock. A true frame rate of 30fps would mean that after 1 hour (30x3600s),108000 frames would have been shot. At 29.97fps after a true hour, 107892 frames have been shot. The discrepancy is nearly 4s. Drop frame deals with that not by dropping frames as it sounds but adjusting the time code so that 1hr of shooting at 29.97fps coincides with 1 hr against the clock. It makes no difference to video quality at all. In editing software, which counts time by frames, it doesn't make any difference whether you use **Drop Frame** or not. In reality the time discrepancy is so small as to be unnoticeable. However, if you are synchronizing sound or video with someone who is using **Drop Frame**, shooting for TV broadcast or even just a stickler for accuracy, it is there for you

Count Up

• **Rec Run** starts the **Time Code** when you press the record button and stops when you stop recording. Thus, every video clip you shoot has a **Time Code** duration the same as the length of time you shoot. That is logical and the most used setting

- **Free Run** starts the **Time Code** the first time you press the record button but carries on recording time whether you are shooting or not. This is of use when shooting with more than one camera. Let's say you are shooting a band. You have one camera set up to record a wide view of the whole band on stage. The **Time Code** starts. At the same time you start a hand held camera with **Free Run**. When you want to cut from the general view on the stand camera to a close-up on the hand held in post editing, you have a definite indication of where to drop from one to the other

Starting Time
- **Reset** zeroes the **Time Code** so a 10 second clip starts at 00:00:00:00 and finishes at 00:00:10:00
- **Manual** simply starts the code at whatever time you choose with the last 2 digits, the fps count at 00

• **Current Time** sets the video to start at whatever time is set on your camera. So if it is 12:33:15, your video will show a start time of 12:33:15:00

Note: In general for standalone video, **Reset** is convenient to simply start with everything at zero

(fig 3)

Sets whether sound is recorded along with video or not.

(fig 1)HDMI Output
Output Mode
• **Monitor Mode** shows the shooting information overlaid on the video on the external monitor
• **Record Mode** send what is known as clean output to the external device. That is to say, you see just the scene you are shooting, no info

Rec Bit

If connected via **HDMI** to an external device with recording capability, when you press the **Rec** button on the camera it will trigger the external device as well.

Time Code

If set **On** the time code from your camera is sent to the external device.

Playback Menu

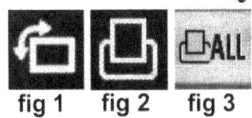

fig 1   fig 2   fig 3

(fig 1) (Rotation)

Off, if you are holding the camera in the landscape plane, you will need to turn it to view a picture shot in portrait orientation. This does mean that you see it at the full dimensions of the screen, however. If rotation is **On** a portrait image is displayed in the landscape plane with black bands either side. A portrait picture viewed in landscape plane will display considerably smaller but you avoid having to turn the camera.

Edit

Sel. Image

Find the image you want to **Edit** and press **OK**. A menu appears.
• **RAW Data Edit** If you have selected a RAW file to edit, a JPG

copy is made for you to work on and a new dialog box comes up

• **Current** This applies current settings to the JPG copy made. As an example, shoot a **RAW** file in 4:3 Aspect Ratio, which will be 5184x3888px. Now go the **SCP** and set **Aspect Ratio** to 16:9, **Saturation** +2. Hit **Edit** and **Current**. You will now have your original **RAW** file and a **JPG** copy according to your **SCP** settings

• **Custom 1/ Custom 2** These enable you to set regularly desired parameters by pressing the right arrow key. When you select a **RAW** file and apply **Custom#** to it, the previously set parameters will be recalled and applied

• **ART BKT** check this to Select an image and you are presented with the range of Art Filters available. Press **OK** and the selected **Art Filters** are applied to your image and saved.

Select 5 filters and you will have 6 images, your original and 5 JPGs with the **Art Effects** applied to them
- **No** simply returns you to the dialog if you have picked the wrong image or don't want to proceed
- **JPG Edit** if you have selected a JPG image to edit you will see a wide range of adjustments you can make. Including cropping and a change to aspect ratio, they are all self-explanatory and show you the results on screen before committing. The original image is retained. If you look anything like me, I can recommend the e-portrait setting

Image Overlay

This is a really interesting facility. Pick 2 or 3 images and combine them for what can be fascinating results. The original images are retained. **Note: Image Overlay** only operates on **RAW** images. After you have chosen the images and the

'Busy' progress bar has gone, you can alter the brighness of each image relative to the other using the arrow keys before committing to the merging. **Note:** you can extract a still from a movie sequence - albeit a 4K (not C4K) image only.

• Select the movie with the still you want

• **Press OK→In-Movie Image Capture→OK**

• Using the arrow keys, find the frame you wish to extract and press **OK** (you can **trim** a movie in a similar manner

Print Order

If you have a suitable **DPOF** (Digital Print Order Format) printer you can connect the camera to it with the USB cable supplied and from **Print Order** select the images you wish to print. Or take the SD card into a print shop that supports **DPOF**.

• **(fig 2)** Press **OK** and find the image you wish to print. On the top right you will see to set the number of prints you want of the image. On pressing **OK** you are offered the choice of adding the **Date** and **Time** taken to be printed on the picture. You can repeat this for each image you want printed
• **(fig 3)** As above but sets each image to have one print made

Reset Protect

If you have **Protected** images on your card this will remove protection from all of them at one go. Useful when you have transferred your images to computer storage and simply wish to clear the card.

Reset Share Order

If you have images set for sharing with your mobile phone, this will cancel all the shares at one go.

Device Connection

First of all install the **OI Share** app. Open it. I find the Olympus connection routine doesn't always work reliably. A more reliable connection can be made by turning on the camera and going through the Connection Setup routine until the QR code comes up. Now go to the phone Connection setting and in the list of available connections you will see E-M5MKIII, followed by some letters and numbers. Select that and the phone will connect to the camera. Go to the app and hit **Remote Control** and you will see the camera view on your screen. You will see the camera listed in your Bluetooth connections too and can connect the same way. The app itself is very well designed and intuitive to use. Using it in landscape orientation gives a good large view.

Custom A1

(fig 1)AF Mode

There is a range of **AF Modes** for every purpose and made even more effective by Olympus's sophisticated on-sensor **PDAF** (Phase Detection Auto Focus), a first on any Micro Four Thirds camera other than Olympus's most expensive flagship cameras.

• **S-AF** Single Auto-Focus. When you press the shutter button, the camera focuses and fires. Each time you press the button the camera refocuses. It sounds slow but in reality the E-M5 Mark III can adjust focus in milliseconds so if your subject is moving towards or away from you at walking pace, **S-AF** will probably still work best

• **C-AF** Continuous Auto-Focus. All the while you hold the shutter in the half-pressed position, the camera will continually adjust focus. When you press the shutter, there is an inevitable small lag before the shutter actually fires and with a fast moving object that lag may be enough for the subject to move out of focus before it is actually recorded. In **C-AF**, the camera computes where the subject will be and adjusts focus accordingly. That is the fundamental difference between **C-AF** and **S-AF**. With **S-AF**, focus is locked when you press the shutter, so if a fast moving subject has moved 2 metres in that time, focus will be off. That begs the question, why not use **C-AF** all the time then? You could but the fact is that on static or slow moving subjects, **S-AF** will lock on faster. **C-AF** works fastest and most reliably when a subject is moving in a predictable manner. That is often true in sport. But if you are photographing your toddler running around in the garden, their movement is no more predictable than their temper. **C-AF** will probably predict wrongly. Since toddlers don't move at high speed by camera standards, **S-AF** will be more likely to nail focus. With C-AF it can become confused with erratic movement and spend a while before finding its bearings. Which to use? Basically, if you find **S-AF** not working well, try **C-AF**. But there's no hard and fast point at which one is better than the other because the things we photograph vary so much. It is a matter of experience and judgement. Of course, if you are planning to shoot sequences or bursts of frames as you would in a typical sports shoot, **C-AF** is the method to use

• **MF** Manual Focus. Once upon a time it was the only way to focus but autofocus has improved so much that it is now rarely used. There are still

occasions, though, when it is the quickest and most reliable way. Imagine you are photographing a bird in a tree. You move around to get a clear view of it through the entanglement of branches and leaves. The only AF area setting usable is **Single Target** because the larger **5** and **9 Target Groups** may focus on nearer leaves or branches while **All Targets** and cannot read your mind and select the bird as a target from among the surrounding greenery. With **Manual Focus** and the superb EVF of the camera you can just turn that focus ring until you have sharp focus. And you don't have to rely on your eye alone because **MF Assist** (Custom, A3) gives you two superb focusing aids in **Focus Peaking** and **Magnify**
• **S-AF+MF** Single Autofocus plus Manual Focus. This setting combines **S-AF** and **MF**. Using **S-AF** alone, turning the lens focusing ring will

have no effect since focus is set by half pressing the shutter release. With this set, you can autofocus any time by half pressing the shutter and then focus manually to modify the autofocus. There is an argument for using this as standard but since Micro Four Thirds lenses tend to be small, you are often touching the focus ring as part of your left hand's grip on the camera/ lens. The Autofocus having done its job, you can easily accidentally knock the focus ring and defocus it a little. A great use for **S-AF+MF** is the bird in a dense tree scenario I mentioned under **MF**. You half press the shutter get ballpark focus and then correct manually for the partly hidden bird

• **C-AF+TR** Continuous Autofocus plus Tracking. Point the camera at your subject, half press the shutter and a green square appears at the focus point. If you now move the camera around or walk towards or away from your subject, focus will be maintained on your subject and you will see the green square moving around, staying on your subject. If focus is lost the green square turns red and you must refocus. Again, you could ask why not use this all the time? The answer is that it can be easily confused if something passes in front of the focused subject and if tracking is lost it is quite slow to manually re-establish it. Ultimately it is simply less flexible and less reliable than **C-AF**, needing large amounts of computing power which can stretch even the E-M5 Mark III. An ideal use for **C-AF+TR** is when photographing a singer on stage because their movement will be within the restricted area of the stage or close to a microphone. I have used it successfully to photograph a fast moving cyclist but you need to set

tracking to their face while they are quite close to the camera so that the focus has enough detail to lock on
• **Preset MF** You need to set a **Fn** button to **Preset MF** to use this. To set the distance, first set the mode to **Preset MF**
• Press **OK** to take you to the SCP
• With Preset MF highlighted, press **OK**
• Press **Info** and manually focus where you wish. You will see the actual distance on screen
• Press **OK** to set that distance. From now on, when you press the **Fn** button to which you have assigned **Preset MF** the camera will jump focus to that distance

Note: If you are using an Olympus lens with the focusing ring clutch you can preset a distance more easily. Pull the clutch back and set focus. Push it forward and the lens will autofocus again. At any time, however, you can pull back the focus clutch and the focus distance will be where you previously set it

(fig 1)AEL/AFL

This determines the function of the **AEL/AFL** button (inside the **Fn Lever**) as it interacts with the shutter button. It operates differently according to the focus mode. To use it, frame the subject and press the button. A green flag comes up on screen to indicate that exposure or focus is locked.

S-AF

• **Mode1** frame your scene. Exposure and focus are locked by a half press of the shutter. All the time you keep the shutter half pressed, exposure and focus remain locked. This is the way most photographers work. If you want exposure and focus for a person at the edge of the frame, point the camera at them and half press the shutter, thus setting focus and exposure. All the time you keep the shutter half pressed, focus and exposure will remain the same. Now reframe the picture with your subject at the edge and press the shutter. If at any time you press **AEL/AFL** button, exposure will be locked at that point and a half press on the shutter button will only change the focus

• **Mode2** - When you half press the shutter, focus is set but exposure is determined at the moment the shutter fires. A press on the **AEL/AFL** again locks the exposure while focusing is done as normal

• **Mode3** - removes the focusing function from the shutter button entirely. Exposure is set by half pressing the shutter button but focusing only occurs when you press the **AEL/AFL** button. Thus, once having pressed the **AEL/AFL** button, focus remains set there until it is pressed again

For general purpose use, **Mode1** is the most intuitive for most photographers.

C-AF

• **Mode1** half press sets the exposure and initiates focusing. Pressing the **AEL/AFL** locks the exposure but focusing continues unaffected

• **Mode2** half pressing the shutter initiates **C-AF**. A full press sets the exposure and focus. Pressing the **AEL/AFL** button locks the exposure

• **Mode3** half pressing the shutter sets the exposure, fully pressing then sets the focus. However, focusing only takes place while the **AEL/AFL** is pressed. This is the back button focusing favoured by sports and wildlife photographers. If you are using **AF-C** to keep focus on a player, when someone runs between him and the camera, it will try to refocus on the nearer blocking player. When your target player is in view again, the

camera will have to start focusing all over again. The re-acquisition of focus that often the slowest part of **C-AF**. However, since the **AEL/AFL** button is controlling focusing, if you stop pressing it when the view is blocked, it stops focusing at the moment you stop pressing. When your chosen player is visible gain, press the button to resume focusing where you left off
• **Mode4** is the same as **Mode3** but exposure is set at the very instant you take the picture rather than while the shutter is half pressed. I find this setting the most logical

Note: on the Olympus Pro lens range, there is a **Fn** button on the lens which can be used to start/stop focusing at will.

MF
• **Mode1** a half press sets the exposure. Full press takes the picture. Pressing **AEL/AFL** locks the exposure

- **Mode2** the exposure is set at the moment of taking the picture.
AEL/AFL locks the exposure
- **Mode3** this is a neat hybrid effect. You are set to manual focus but a press on the **AEL/AFL** button focuses the lens. Exposure is set by half pressing the shutter release. A handy way of quickly establishing a starting point for your own focusing. With the E-M5 Mark III's focusing efficiency I don't often find **MF** necessary

AF Scanner

Inevitably there will be circumstances when your E-M5 Mark III will not be able to autofocus. Perhaps the light is too low or the subject has too little contrast. The first thing to do is try to find something light in colour and with adequate contrast as near as possible to your focus point. Perhaps the 5 or 9 point grid will work better. If the camera really cannot focus it

will rack the lens out from closest focus to infinity over and over. Obviously, that achieves nothing. This setting determines what course of action the camera will take when it is stumped.
- **Mode 1** it tries once and gives up
- **Mode2** it tries again
- **Mode3** it carries on no matter what

(fig 1)C-AF Sensitivity

You might think that you need the sensitivity of continuous AutoFocus to be as responsive as possible, so that if subject position changes,**C-AF** will keep up with it. However, there are times when it needs to be lower. Imagine you are photographing football. You are tracking a particular player who has possession of the ball. Another player runs between that player and you. At the highest sensitivity focus immediately transfers to that player and must re-focus on your intended target when you have a clear view again. With lower sensitivity set, the E-M5 Mark III will change focus less readily and will not react to the transitory block of view, keeping focus on your target player. For tennis singles, where you can expect a clear view of the player at all times, the highest sensitivity would be appropriate. Equally, if your are using a centre grid focus pattern and cannot keep it on the subject at all times, a lower sensitivity will stop the camera shifting focus to the background every time you lose track. There's no alternative to experience for finding your best setting but I find that the default 0 is generally usable with bird photography (elusive creatures!) a switch to +5 working well for subjects like racing cars.

(fig 1)C-AF Center Start

When using any of the **C-AF** modes that use a **Target Group**, that is a grid of focus points covering everything from the full screen to a cross shaped cluster in the centre, the camera may well determine the main focus point to be a point somewhere off the centre of the grid. With this set the focus point will always start at the centre of the grid pattern. That usually makes sense since you will most likely centre your subject on screen instinctively. Once initial focus on the centre is established, the focus algorithm takes over. This avoids the situation where you half press the shutter and the camera picks a point of focus at variance with your intent. **Note:** you activate this by ticking the box beside each **Target Group** you wish to include.

Doesn't apply to **C-AF+Tracking** or **Single Target** modes

(fig 1)C-AF Center Priority

When using **Target Groups** other than **All**,(covering the whole screen) for **C-AF**, tick the appropriate boxes to make focus **always** follow the centre of the **Target Group**. It will change focus to another area of the grid only when it cannot focus in the centre of any reason. **Note:** the difference between this and the previous **Center Start** setting is that **Center Priority** will always try to keep focus in the centre while **Center Start** will move it to another area of the grid if it deems it better. **Note: Center Priority** effectively negates the **Center Start** setting in the modes for which it is activated. Unless you have a very unpredictable subject to follow, this mode is likely to be the most effective since you will instinctively centre the **Target Group** on your subject.

Custom A2

fig 1

(fig 1)Mode Settings

It is unlikely that you will use all of the **AF Target** modes, so if you use only **Single** and **All**, untick the others. Now, when you go to change mode on the SCP, for example, you will only your chosen modes.

AF Area Pointer

When correct focus is obtained, it is confirmed by the brief flash of a green blob in the top right of the display. If you wish, it can be confirmed by the appearance of a green box indicating not only correct focus but where that focus is.

• **Off** there is confirmation only by the green blob

• **Mode 1** a green box appears briefly confirming focus and its position

• **Mode 2** is similar to **Mode 1** except the box is in view all the time the shutter is half pressed

Note: if you are using the **All** Target Group, when set to **Mode 2** the screen will show all the areas of your image that are in sharp focus while the shutter button is half pressed.

AF Targeting Pad

While using the EVF you often need to move the **AF Target** away from its customary centre position. You can use the arrow cursor keys to move it around but set this item **On** and you can use your finger on the monitor to shift it around. If you find yourself moving the area around by accident, a double tap on the monitor will toggle it on and off. Very useful If you use the monitor flat against the camera rear rather than folded out, when you may find your nose re-positioning the AF Target by accident!

(fig 1)Set Home

For this to work best, you need to set a **Fn** button to **Home**. It must be one in the list under **Custom Menu B→Button Function**, the topmost item. You most likely have a basic focusing method which suits you. **Set Home** enables you to set that as your default position and recall it immediately no matter what the current **AF** settings are. If you tick **S-AF** and set and tick the target size and position, when you press the designated **Fn** button no matter what the settings, they will return to your **Home** setting. Pressing the **Fn** button again toggles between your **Home** setting and whatever the setting was before you pressed it.

(fig 1)Custom Settings

If you highlight the **AF Area** setting on the **SCP** and press **OK** you can set various parameters using the arrow keys and front and rear dials. I can't see anything wrong with the defaults but if they don't suit you, you can swap them around here. You can set two separate configurations. If you tick **Set 2**, **Info** will toggle between **Set 1** and **Set 2**.

Custom A3

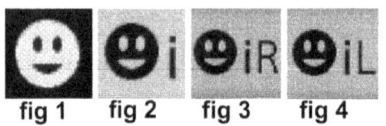

fig 1 fig 2 fig 3 fig 4

AF Limiter

If you were taking pictures at a game of table tennis you might know that the closest a player might come to you would be 2m and the furthest away 4m. It would obviously speed up auto-focusing if the E-M5 Mark III's **PDAF** system knew to limit its scope to those distances. This provided a way to doing that. You can set up 3 predetermined limits.

Release Priority

• **On** you can take a picture even if it will be out of focus

• **Off** the shutter will not fire if the subject will be out of focus

AF Illuminator

The Olympus E-M5 Mark III will find focus in very dim light indeed but there are limits. When the camera judges the light too dim for it focus properly, it will switch on a small but powerful red light. The light stays on only long enough for the camera to find focus and then switches off. **AF Illuminator** is best left on unless circumstances dictate otherwise.

(fig 1)Face Priority

• **Off** Focusing takes place regardless of any faces in shot
• **(fig 1)** If there is a face in shot, the camera will focus on it
• **(fig 2)** If there is a face in shot and eyes are detected, focus will be on the eye nearest the camera
• **(fig 3)** As above but focus on the right eye
• **(fig 4)** As above but focus on the left eye

Note: any face detected is outlined by a white box. if you are using the default Digital ESP metering (you almost certainly will be), the camera will automatically set optimum exposure for the face.

AF Focus Adj.

In the unlikely event that you find your E-M5 Mark III's autofocus is inaccurate you can adjust it here.

• **Default Data** if all your lenses are off focus by a similar amount, you can adjust the overall action of the **PDAF** here. This is most unlikely

• **Lens Data** if you have a focus problem with one or more particular lenses you can set a correction for each one here. You can correct at 25 different positions on the focus grid and pressing **Info** will allow you to correct separately for wide and tele zoom positions. Good luck with that!

Note: to set the correction, focus on a detailed subject (preferably print out a lens test chart) and magnify the image as much as possible. Use a tripod as any movement of the camera will just make the focusing accuracy worse. Let the lens focus using the AF and then carefully move the indicator back and forth to find the optimum position. Press **OK** when done.

Custom A4
Preset MF Distance

You can register a focusing distance here so that when you select **Pre MF** on the SCP, the camera be set to Manual Focus and this distance. This doesn't disable normal **MF**, it just sets it to this distance for a starter. If you focus away from the preset, you will need to select another focus mode and then reselect **Pre MF**.

Note: there is another way to preset the manual focus if you have an Olympus lens with the pull-back collar for engaging **MF**. Pull the collar back and manually focus on the desired distance. Now push it forward again to revert to autofocus. When you pull it back again, it will be focused on where you previously set it.

MF Assist

When using Manual Focusing, the optimum setting can be a little tricky to find sometimes. You can enlist two aids here, which will spring into action when you turn the focusing ring.

• **Magnify** As you turn the focusing ring the image will be magnified. A half press on the shutter button returns you to a normal view. You can choose the level of magnification (up to 14x) using the front or rear dials. At 14x magnification you will be glad of the E-M5 Mark III's excellent stabilization

• **Peaking** This adds coloured lines to edges in the image with the greatest intensity at the sharpest points. A press on the Info button allows you to change the colour and opacity of the lines. My personal preference is to use **Magnify** for stills and **Peaking** for Movie but both are amazingly effective and remove all the uncertainty from manual focusing.

Note: you can also adjust **Peaking** settings in **Custom Menu D3**

MF Clutch

Some of Olympus's range of lenses, notably the Pro series but others as well, have a manual focusing ring which, when slid/ pulled back acts as a clutch, setting the lens to Manual Focus. This action overrides any autofocus setting. It is easy to forget or not see that the collar is slid back and wonder why the lens will not autofocus no matter how you set it. Disabling the clutch obviates that possibility.

Focus Ring

If you came to the E-M5 Mark III from another make of camera it is quite possible that the focusing ring of the previous camera worked in the opposite direction to Olympus lenses. It is infuriatingly difficult to adjust to this change and pictures can be missed as a result. This item allows you to set the focusing ring of the E-M5 Mark III to turn the same way as your previous camera.

Bulb/Time Focusing

When making a long exposure using Bulb or Time exposure you would not normally wish to alter the focus, since it would lead to your subject appearing blurred. There are rare occasions when you might want to alter it during exposure for a special effect and this allows you to do it.

Reset Lens

Normally, when you turn on the E-M5 Mark III the lens will be set to infinity. If you set this item **Off**, if you were focused at 1m when you switched off, you will be focused in 1m when you switch on again.

Custom B

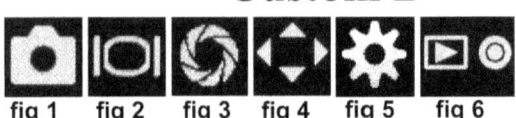

fig 1   fig 2   fig 3   fig 4   fig 5   fig 6

(fig 1)Button Function

The E-M5 Mark III has a dozen or so programmable controls available on the body. All can perform a variety of functions including being disabled. There is also **L-Fn** which is a button button on the barrel of many Olympus lenses. The defaults for these buttons are often the best use of them and I would suggest leaving them as they are at first. If you then find yourself constantly going to the menu to use one particular function, set that to a button. The one that I do change immediately is the (fig 2)**Function** button which by default duplicates the action of the **OK** button in invoking the **SCP**. If you disable **Custom I→EV Auto Switch** you can use it to switch between the EVF and the Monitor. In general, though, I find the **EVF Auto Switching** works well and I set this button to **Bracketing** or **HDR**. The only items that are less than intuitive here are:

• (fig 3) this refers to the small **Fn** button to the right of the lens on the front of the camera body

• (fig 4) **Function** this refers to the arrow keys. You can either set them to bring up the **AF Target Area** or with **Direct Function** use the down and right arrows as extra **Fn** buttons. The left arrow always brings up the **AF Target Area** and the up arrow detailed shooting information

Note: it can be hard to remember how you have customized the buttons and dials. You can get a reminder when shooting by going to (fig 5) on the **SCP** and pressing **OK** which takes you directly to this menu position.

(Fig 6) Function

This sets the function of the **Rec** button when you are in **Playback** mode. The options are

- **Multiple Image Selection** You can go through the images on the monitor and select all or some for a later action, deleting or protecting for example
- **Transfer Preselection** As you press the **Rec** button on each image you will see the 'Share' icon appear. If you set it up on the Olympus phone app, the chosen images will be automatically transferred to the phone when the app is started

(fig 1)Dial Function

You can set the function of the front and rear dials in different modes, including when using the menu and in **Playback**. **M/B** means Manual/Bulb, by the way.

Dial Direction

If turning the front or rear dials one way or the other to increase/decrease a parameter feels more natural to you can set it here.,

(fig 1)Fn Lever Function

This one is quite complicated! It operates in conjunction with whatever you have set the dials to do in **Dial function**, earlier in this menu.

• **Mode1** the lever functions to change the settings to your choice in **Dial Settings**

• **Mode2** you can switch between 2 focus settings. You can change any or all of **AF Mode**, **AF Target** and **AF Area**. Which you change are set by the tick boxes accessed to the right of **Mode2**. Having switched to **Mode2**, set the **Fn Lever** to position 1. Go to the the **SCP** and set the focus settings you want. Now, switch the **Fn Lever** to position 2 and set a second set of focus settings. Now, when the Fn Lever is set to **Mode2** it will toggle between these two settings

• **Mode3** position 1 functions as set in **Dial Settings** but Position 2 puts the camera directly into **Movie** mode, as if you had turned the **Mode** dial to **Movie Note:** in **Mode 2**, if when set to either position, you change the focus settings, those become the new switchable ones. Thus if you set the lever to Position 1 as **S-AF** and Position 2 as **C-AF**, if while using Position 1 you set **MF**, that will be your new Position 1 setting. If you switch off or change **Mode** setting, when you switch back on or return to **Mode2** the last used settings will be recalled

Fn Lever/Power Lever

If for some reason you would prefer to power the camera on and off with the **Fn Lever** rather than the dedicated switch provided, this allows you to do so. You can even choose which position is **On** or **Off**.

(fig 1)Elec. Zoom Speed

 Some lenses, for example the Olympus 12-50mm have a power zoom facility, useful for video in particular because of its smoothness. This setting enables you to choose how quickly the lens will traverse its zoom range in **Stills** mode. It is set separately for Video in the Video menu.

Custom C1

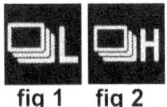
fig 1   fig 2

S-AF Release Priority

This gives you the choice of what happens when you press the shutter release but the camera has not yet locked focus on the subject.

• **On** The shutter will release regardless of the state of focus

• **Off** If the camera does not have sharp focus, the shutter will not release

Note: As an ex press photographer, I deem it more important to capture an image than whether it is pin sharp or not. For more leisured types of work, focus will be more important. No-one wants an out of focus landscape picture. The reality is that the E-M5 Mark III focuses so fast and accurately that this setting raraely makes any difference.

C-AF Release Priority

As with **S-AF** (above) but I'd suggest leaning towards the **On** setting since focus will always be less certain with **C-AF**, particularly with a fast moving subject. It would be a shame to miss a good action picture simply bcause focus was a little off the mark.

(fig 1)Settings

This sets the parameters for the **L** sequence Setting. If you use the **Silent Shutter** you can get up to 10fps as opposed to the 6fps maximum of the mechanical/hybrid setting. The beauty of the **L Settings** is that the camera will focus separately for each frame, maintaining focus throughout your sequence. All of these allow you to limit the number of frames in a sequence. I can't see much reason to do this. You will know when the camera is nearing its limits when the shooting speed starts to slow down. **Pro Capture** gives you up to 30fps but not **C-AF**. Focus remains where it was when you first pressed the release. The **Pre-Shutter Frames** setting is remarkable. When the shutter release button is half pressed, the camera starts taking pictures. When you press it fully it records for as long as you hold it down. When you let go of the release, the E-M5 Mark III retains the sequence you have shot plus up to 14 frames from before you pressed it. Thus, if you are waiting for a bird to come to its nest, if you half press the shutter while waiting and then fully press it as soon as possible after the bird appears, you will be certain to capture all the action. Given the speed of birds, it is almost certain that even a fast reaction on the part of the photographer would have missed some of the action.

(fig 2)Settings

These settings allow for higher sequence speeds but at the expense of real time focusing. Usually **L Sequence** will be more useful. The main difference is that you can get 10fps with the mechanical shutter. **Pro Capture** on the **H Sequence** setting allows you a choice of lower speeds rather than 30fps or nothing. All in all, you'll probably use **L Sequence** for everything in **C-AF** with **H Sequence** coming in to its own only when you want the highest speeds from the mechanical shutter. No follow focusing, though.

Flicker Reduction

Under artificial light you may encounter flickering effects. This will be due to a clash between your shutter speed and the electric mains frequency.

- **Anti-Flicker LV** Here you can set 50 or 60Hz as appropriate to your area or have the camera set the best one automatically
- **Anti-Flicker Shooting** Sets whether anti-flicker comes into play at all. Switch this on only if you have a flicker problem

Custom C2

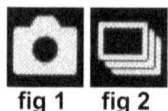
fig 1   fig 2

(fig 1)Image Stabilizer

The **IBIS** (**I**n **B**ody **I**mage **S**tabilization of the E-M5 Mark III at 5.5 stops over a non-stabilized camera. The rule of thumb formula for the shutter speed necessary for a given lens with 35mm cameras was that it should match the lens. Thus, a 50mm lens would need a minimum shutter speed of 1/50th to get sharp blur free results. Micro Four Thirds cameras with their smaller sensor halve the angle of view of any given lens, effectively doubling the magnification, so a 50mm lens needs 50x2, a minimum shutter speed of 1/100th. A 25mm lens would need 1/50th and so on. With the stabilization on this camera, I can hold a 150mm lens reliably still at

1/25th!

- **Off** is for when the camera is mounted on a tripod or solid base. There is a possibility that when the camera is firmly mounted stabilization can cause 'drifting' or slight blurring of the image
- **S-IS1** the normal setting. The stabilization functions in all directions
- **S-IS2** if you are panning a subject while holding the camera in landscape orientation This setting applies stabilization vertically only, so that the camera does not interpret your swinging the camera along with your subject as unwanted camera movement
- **S-IS3** does the same job as above but when you are panning the camera while holding it in portrait orientation
- **S-IS AUTO** decides for itself what you are doing and stabilizes accordingly. I always feel that it might

misinterpret and prefer to set the **S-IS1** mode myself though I have no evidence that it makes any difference

Note: panning is moving the camera horizontally while keeping the subject in the same spot on the screen for a classic blurred background/ sharp subject sports effect)

(fig 2) Image Stabilizer

This applies specifically when you are shooting in any sequence mode with stabilization on. Stabilization takes a lot of computing power as does sequence shooting, especially with **C-AF**. You can decide here what is most important to you.

• **IS Priority** this will slow down the sequence in order to make sure the stabilization is effective

• **Fps Priority** this will keep the sequence speed up, allowing some camera shake if necessary

Note: Usually when you are shooting a sequence, it will be of a fast moving subject in which case you will need a high shutter speed to prevent subject motion blur. Over about 1/750th stabilization is unnecessary or even, in theory, detrimental, in which case you can free up processor cycles by turning stabilization **Off** (see previous item)

Half Way Release With IS

With this **Off**, stabilization is applied to the image for the instant the picture is taken. Set **On**, stabilization is effective from when you half press the shutter button through to firing. The effect is startling, especially with long telephoto lenses. One moment the scene looks jerky and moves about in the finder, then as you half press the shutter it is as if a giant clamp has been applied to it. The only downside to **Half Way Rls With IS** is that it uses more battery power but that is a small price to pay in my view. Of course, if you have ultra-steady hands, you could prolong battery life by turning this off and still have the benefit of stabilization.

Lens I.S. Priority

This tells the camera what to do if you mount a lens with its own stabilization on the E-M5 Mark III. It is for use mainly with Panasonic Micro Four Thirds lenses, many of which have their own stabilization built in. If you set it **On** the camera will disable its **IBIS** and use the lens's stabilization instead. There's no point since the E-M5 Mark III **IBIS** will always be better. **Note:** some Olympus lenses have their own stabilization too. When these are fitted the camera automatically uses the lens and body stabilization in combination for even better results. If you really do want to use Panasonic lens stabilization, switch the **IBIS Off** (see previous item) and make sure the lens stabilization is **On**.

Custom D1

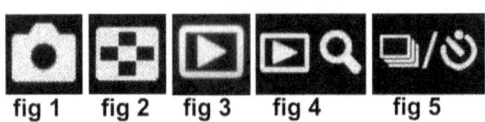
fig 1 fig 2 fig 3 fig 4 fig 5

(fig 1)Control Settings

This sets what happens when you press the **OK** button. Most photographers find that the easiest way to make a change to a shooting parameter on the fly is the well implemented **SCP**, **S**uper **C**ontrol **P**anel. Change from 200 ISO to 1600 ISO? Just hit **OK**, touch the ISO panel and turn the rear dial. However, you might prefer the **Live Control** which leaves with a view of your subject while you make a change. With **Live Control**, you select your parameter to change with the rear dial and scroll through the options with the front dial. **Control Settings** lets you tailor the **OK** button function. In the P/A/S/M shooting modes, with both boxes unticked, pressing the **OK** button brings up a list of your current settings. It is not active and you cannot make adjustments from it. If you tick one box, you get **Live Control** or **SCP** as selected, of course. If you tick both boxes, pressing **INFO** toggles between them. It's a little pointless leaving both boxes unticked since pressing **Info** brings up your current settings anyway. For **Auto** you have an extra option of **Live Guide** which brigs up a short list of the settings you can change in **Auto** including some shooting tips! For **Art** toy have the extra option of **Art Menu** which brings up a selectable list of all the **Art** modes available. All of these **Control Settings** work the same way, you use **INFO** button to run through each item ticked. Ditto **SCN**.

(fig 2)Info Settings

Just as you can tailor **OK** button options, so you can tailor the **INFO** button here. The

(fig 3)Playback Info

This setting controls what happens when you press the **INFO** while reviewing images. All unticked, the button does nothing. As you tick more boxes, a press on the **INFO** button when reviewing will step through them. They options are pretty straightforward. **Overall** gives you a histogram of the colour components of your image and the shooting information. **Highlights and Shadow** gives you a flashing display of which picture areas are clipped, that is do not contain detail, being beyond the camera's ability to capture them at the exposure used. **Light Box** gives you a way to compare two images side by side.

Get the image you want on screen and press **Info** until a split screen comes up. On the left will be a section of the image you selected and on the right the next image taken. Scroll through your images using the left and right arrow keys or the front dial until you find the one you want to compare. Turning the rear dial will magnify both images.

(fig 4)Playback

 This is only relevant if you have a **Fn** button set to In **Playback** mode, if you press that **Fn** button it will scroll through the screens you have set here. If you set them tick them all, the first press shows you the area you to be magnified and allows you to move the frame about to set which area will be magnified and by how much. You can move the frame with your finger and set the magnification with the rear dial. The nest press shows you the magnified section of the image as you previously set it. The next press lets you scroll through the other recorded images at the magnification and area set. You can vary magnification here if you wish but not the area magnified.

LV-Info

This sets what you will see when you press the **Info** button while shooting pictures. All boxes unticked gives you a screen with all the shooting information shown. Tick **Image Only** and you can toggle between the default screen and a clean image only screen. You will see the most basic shooting settings when you touch the shutter button but they will disappear after a few seconds after you take your finger from the shutter button. **Image Only** is a necessity for distraction free composition. There are 2 further screens that can be added and stepped through by presses on the

Info button. The choices on both these screen are the same, **Histogram** which is an aid to getting the best exposure for a given scene, **Highlight and Shadow** which will show you areas of your image where clipping is occurring, that is to say areas beyond the scope of the camera to record with detail and **Level Gauge**. You can add all three of these to one screen but on top the information already on the Info screen, you may find it rather cluttered. So, if you tick both **Custom** screens and set **Level Gauge** on **Custom** 1 and **Histogram** on **Custom** 2 other they will show on separate screens one after the other.

(fig 2)Settings

If you go to **Playback** mode and turn the rear dial one click clockwise, you are presented with a grid view of all your images. This menu item lets you set how many images are presented to you at once plus, with further turns of the dial, which other screen you see (or not). If you have shot any **My Clips**, the time limited short video sequences, they can by viewed separately from still images and **Calendar** lets you select a date and see what images you made that day.

Picture Mode Settings

There are 40 or so **Picture Modes** (effects, really) available, from **i-Enhance** through **Pinhole** to **Instant Film**. If you regularly use only a few of these it is a pain to have to scroll though all of them to find the one you want. Untick the redundant ones here and when you go to **Picture Mode** from the menu or from the **SCP** you need only choose from your favourites.

(fig)Settings

There are a bewildering number of shutter/shooting settings available. For example, if you want a 2 second delayed action, you must choose which of the three shutter modes you wish to use with it. You are unlikely to use all of these so this provides a way of cutting down on the scrolling necessary to find the one you want.

Multi Function Settings

If you have set a button to **Multi Function**, this sets the functions it will make available. For **Multi Function** to work, it must be set to a button in **Custom B→Button Function**. It is invoked by pressing the button down and turning the rear dial at the same time. A list of parameters appears along the bottom of the screen. Select one and the button is now set to that. Thus, select **Image Aspect** and let go. Now, when you press the chosen button, the **Image Aspect** parameters come up and can be selected.

Custom D2

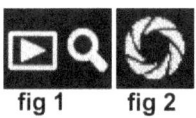

fig 1   fig 2

Live View Boost
Manual Shooting

In normal shooting the camera gives you a view of the subject that reflects what the recorded image will look like. In very dim light, though, the view may be too dark and jerky to comfortably examine and frame on screen. **Live View Boost** tries to improve that situation in various shooting modes.

• **On1** Tries to lessen the jerkiness of the viewing

• **On2** Tries to brighten the view

Note: when set to **Off** you are viewing the image as it will be recorded. **On1** and **On2** will not reflect the image as it will be recorded. In all three cases, the recorded image will be exactly the same, of course. You can apply the

Live View Boost in any stills mode I but would question its use in **Manual** and **Live Composite** since the purpose of those is to give you direct access to the effect of your camera settings on the image

Art LV Mode

The **Art** filters put a heavy load on even the E-M5 Mark III's processing power. Turning a live view of a scene into a representation of a water colour on the fly is no mean feat. This setting lets you choose between an accurate view of your **Art** picture or a better viewing experience.

• **Mode1** gives you an accurate view which may be flickery or jerky

Mode2 lightens the art effect in order to give you a smoother viewing experience **Note:** Only the viewing is altered, the **Art** effect will be applied to image as you have set it.

LV Close Up Settings
If you have set a **Fn** button to **Magnify** his sets how the enlarged view behaves.

LV Close Up Mode

• **Mode1** when you press the **Fn** button a green frame showing the area which will be magnified appears. Press the button again and the magnified view appears. When you half press the shutter button the view reverts to the full frame and focusing takes place

• **Mode2** as **Mode1** but having invoked the magnified area, focusing takes place while still magnified. To revert to the full frame, press the **Fn** button again. The advantage of this mode is that by focusing in an enlarged view, you can be more precise about where the camera should focus

Note: the green box showing the area that will be magnified can be moved around the screen using the arrow keys or via the touchscreen. To get rid of the **Magnify** box, touch the small **Off** icon on the left side of the screen.

Live View Boost

Set **On** the magnified image is rendered brighter, useful in dim conditions. The boost affects only the viewed image, not the recorded one.

(fig 1)Default Settings

When you view an image in **Playback** it is first displayed at full frame. If you turn the rear dial one click right, it magnifies the image. This sets the initial magnification invoked by the dial.

(fig 2)Settings

(fig 2)Lock

• **Off**, press the button to see the preview, let it go to revert to normal view. **On**, press it to see the preview and press it again to revert to normal view

Live View Boost

When in **Preview** to view the depth of field, this will boost the image brightness for easier viewing.

Custom D3
Grid Settings

A grid, a series of fine lines superimposed on the monitor and/or EVF can be very helpful in composition or any type of technical photography where precision of placement is important.

Display Colour

You can preset 2 flavours of grid for quick access with full control over colour (**RGB**), **0 0 0** being black **255 255 255** being white and **255 0 0** being red. I find **128 128 128** and Opacity **50%** suitable. That graphic is actually Alpha, first letter of the Greek alphabet and is used to mean opacity in computer graphics. I suppose it is no surprise to see Greek letters used on a camera called Olympus!

Displayed Grid

Choose your preferred type of grid here.

Apply Settings to EVF

On sets the grid set here to show on both the monitor and the EVF. If this is set **Off** the grid appears only on the monitor. In that case, in **Custom→I→EVF Grid Settings** you can set a grid purely for the EVF. This makes it possible to show a grid on the monitor only, the EVF only or both at once. The EVF grid can thus be a different colour and opacity to the one on the monitor.

Peaking Settings

 Peaking is a focusing aid which applies a highlight to in focus edge areas of the subject. It only operates in **MF** and can be used at the same time as the **Magnify** facility of you want. The highlights tell you not only whether you are in focus or not but which over parts of the picture are in the same focusing plane and will be in sharp focus.

Peaking Color

You have a choice of red, yellow, black or white highlights. I find red the easiest to judge.

Highlight Intensity

this basically makes the peaking highlights thicker or thinner.

Image Brightness Adj.

This boosts the image brightness in low light situations where the peaking may be difficult to make out. It only lightens the image on screen, not affecting the recorded image at all.

Histogram Settings

You are unlikely to need to change the default **0 - 255** setting. The **Histogram** provides a good guide to the proper exposure of an image but needs experience to understand and use. The X axis, is set to 0 (no light, black) on the left to 255 (fully exposed, white) on the right. The height of the histogram shows the proportion of pixels of a given brightness in your image. A classic average image shows what looks like a hill rising in the centre, tapering off each side evenly to the extreme X axis sides. If you see the peak to the right, it means there is a higher distribution of light pixels, to the left a higher proportion of dark pixels. You would only need to alter this setting if somewhere in your workflow there was a limitation on the brightness range that could be accommodated and you wished to stay within that range when shooting. Altering this doesn't change the recorded image in any way.**Note:** the main use for this would be in video but it affects how software handles the brightness range, not the brightness range of your image or video.

Mode Guide

When you turn the **Mode** dial, this tells you what the camera will do. Thus turn it to **S** and the camera reminds you to **set the shutter speed manually**. The message lasts for a few seconds or until you touch the shutter release.

Selfie Assist

When you fold out the monitor and hold the camera facing towards you it reverses the viewing image so that framing is more intuitive. It brings up a little camera icon at the bottom of the monitor. Move the green focus area box where you want it. A touch on the camera icon focuses and fires the shutter after a one second delay. You can set a delayed action mode if you want a longer delay and/or more than one shot taken per shutter push. If you want the ultimate Selfie, set the camera to **iAuto** and **e-Portrait**.

This will make you look like a supermodel and while it may not do much for, say the Grand Canyon behind you, this a is a Selfie so lets get our priorities right :-)

Custom D4

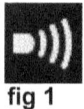
fig 1

(fig 1)
If you don't like the little beep that sounds when the focus locks on, this will turn it off. Handy in very quiet environments where the noise can irritate other people but in general use I like audio confirmation that focus is found.

HDMI
This controls what happens when the **HDMI** connection is plugged in to a TV. You can play back or monitor using this connection.

Output Size
Set this to match the TV's **HDMI** setting. All current TVs will support modes up to 1080p. If the TV doesn't support **4K** or **C4K**, it won't attempt to show it. The overall working of this is more dependent on your TV's

settings and facilities than the camera's but most TVs now will be **1080p**

HDMI Control

If your TV has a remote control that supports it, switching this **On** allows control of the E-M5 Mark III's output from the remote, Again, this is down to your TV more than the camera.

Output Frame Rate

Set this to your TV's frame rate. In general, 60fps for the USA, 50fps for Europe. Modern TVs will cope either way.

USB Mode

This sets how the camera connects to a printer or computer.

• **Auto** The camera will ask you to choose which option you require when you plug the USB cable in and connect to a printer or computer

• **Storage** The camera is seen by the computer as a disk drive, no different to taking the SD card out and plugging it into a card reader. I find it faster and more robust than **MTP**

• **MTP** Stands for **M**edia **T**ransfer **P**rotocol. Instead of your camera showing up as Removable Disk D: in your file explorer or whatever, it shows up as E-M5 Mark III Digital Camera

• **PCM Recorder** with this on and the **USB** connected to an Olympus (external) PCM Recorder, the camera will trigger the recorder on and off in sync with the camera

Custom E1
Exposure Shift

 Correct exposure is to some extent a matter of preference more than an objective measurement. If you find that the camera is, in your eyes, consistently yielding results too light or too dark, you can bring it in line with your taste here. There is a separate adjustment for the three metering modes. It's unlikely that you would want to make more than a ½ stop adjustment here because digital camera auto-exposure is a pretty fine art these days.

EV Step

 This affects the amount by which the controls step through shutter speed, aperture and exposure compensation. Set to **1/3EV**, if your shutter speed is 1/60th and you turn the dial to alter it, it goes 1/60, 1/80, 1/100, 1/125th. Set it to **1/2EV** and you have 1/60, 1/90, 1/125. **1EV** gives you 1/60, 1/125th. I find 1/2EV enough while avoiding too much dial twiddling.

ISO Step

This affects the steps for **ISO**. You can choose **1/3EV** or **1EV** depending on your taste for granular control or fast change.

ISO-Auto Set

This is a crucial control when you use **Auto ISO**.

Upper Limit/Default

Set the **High Limit** to the highest **ISO** that you consider has acceptable noise levels for the kind of photography you like to do. For a landscape photographer who want maximum detail/ least noise this might be 800 ISO. For a live music or action photographer this might be 6400 ISO. **Default** is essentially the minimum **ISO** the camera will use. I find 3200 and 200 ISO work for me. No matter what you set here, if a correct exposure cannot be made within your settings, the camera will override them.

Lowest S/S

This sets how far down the camera will set the shutter speed before it starts to raise the **ISO** in **ISO Auto**. It operates on **P** and **A** modes. If you are photographing sports you might set this to 1/500th but on a static evening scene and taking full advantage of the **IBIS** with a 25mm lens you might set it to 1/10th so that as the light falls the camera will keep shooting at your **Default** as long as possible

ISO-Auto

The main use for this is to set whether **Auto ISO** will operate in Manual Mode.

• **P**, **A** or **S Auto ISO** will operate in those modes but not **Manual**. That is logical since **Manual** control implies that you are making the settings, not the camera, and will therefore wish to use set the **ISO** to your preference for that shot

• **All Auto ISO** works in **M** mode too. Lets say you are shooting your child running around with a ball in the garden. You know you need a certain shutter speed to prevent motion blur and a certain aperture to give enough depth of field. You set the camera to 1/500th @ f/5.6. In **A**, if the light changes beyond what **Auto-ISO** can cope with, the camera will alter the shutter speed to keep exposure correct. It may be slower than you want giving you blurred results. In **S**, the camera will alter the aperture if the light drops beyond the **Auto-ISO** settings and you may not have enough depth of field. Set to **All**, in **M** mode having set your parameters 500th @ f/5.6 they will stay set and the camera will alter only the **ISO** to keep the exposure correct. You will need to set a wide **ISO** range under **ISO-Auto Set** as this setting does allows your image to be badly exposed if the light goes outside of your **ISO-Auto Set** limitations

Noise Filter

This sets the amount of noise reduction that is employed at higher **ISO** settings. At high **ISO** settings noise is just a fact of photography. However, you can do some noise reduction in camera by setting this **Noise Filter**. It only works for shooting **JPG**, not **RAW** files. The 3 levels offered are well chosen with even **High** not making the image look too smeary. The downside of applying the **Noise Filter** in camera is that the detail lost is lost for good. It is better practice to shoot with the **Noise Filter Off** and do the reduction in post processing, where you can do it on a copy.

Nonetheless, the noise reducing techniques implemented by Olympus do the job efficiently and you may well find it perfectly good for your purposes. **Note:** one effective way to lower image noise is to reduce the pixel count. If you are going to view the image on a tablet, for example, reducing image size by 50% in post processing will lose a lot of noise along he way.

Noise Reduct.

During a long exposure random noise in the form of bright pixels is generated by the sensor itself. It is generated even at low ISO settings and is different in character from high ISO noise. The camera identifies this noise by making a blank exposure at the given shutter speed immediately after your picture is taken and comparing it with your image. It then computes what the pixel probably should be (interpolation) and replaces the noise pixel with that. The downside of this technique is that if you make a 60 second exposure, the camera will take another 60 seconds on top to work its magic so your 1 minute exposure turns into 2 minutes. The options here are **Off** which can leave you with a flawed picture, **On** which goes through the noise reduction routine even on normal exposures, completely unnecessary and time wasting or **Auto**, far and away the best choice. In practice, **Auto** only operates on images with exposure times 4 seconds or longer, in other words, when it becomes necessary.

Custom E2
Bulb/Time Timer

This dictates the maximum time for which you can expose in **Bulb** or **Time**. The longest timed shutter speed on the E-M5 Mark III is 60 seconds. However, if you set the mode dial to **B**ulb you can set longer exposures than 60 seconds. **Bulb** and **Time** differ in that with **Bulb** you press the shutter and hold it down for as long as you wish to expose. With **Time** you press the shutter button once to start the exposure, then the shutter stays open until you press again. While you can regulate the exposure by pressing the shutter button, therefore, **Bulb/Time Timer** allows you to apply a time to them. Set it to 30 minutes and you have in effect set a shutter speed of 30 minutes.

Bulb/Time Monitor

You will be using **Bulb** or **Time** in low light conditions. If it is difficult to see the subject, you can brighten the monitor view here. It will not affect the recorded image.

Live Bulb

See **Live Time** below.

Live Time

While making your long exposure it is useful to get an idea of how it is building. In the past with **Bulb** or **Time** exposures, the screen went blank while the picture was taken so you could only see the result at the end of the exposure. The **Live** element here means that you may take a peek at the image several times as it is being built up. The number of peeks you are allowed is limited, however as it can impinge on image quality. For that reason, the lower the ISO, the more peeks you can have. The setting here is the interval between screen updates.

This is quite a facility to have because if you judge an exposure of 8 minutes at /5.6 with a screen update every 30 seconds, if the image is to your liking at the 10th update, you can press th shutter button again and end the exposure. The panel that opens up at the bottom left of the display is a histogram, built up as the exposure progresses. Since the first period of time will be the image building up from nothing, the pixel distribution will all be to the left, the shadow side. As the image builds, the histogram will move to the right. Because night photographs usually have contrasty lighting from small sources like street lamps a histogram will rarely look like the classic 'normal' exposure one of a central hill tapering off to the sides and the monitor image is a better criterion.

Composite Settings

Composite here refers to adding elements of the developing **Time** image exposure to the to the image so far. Thus, if there is a street lamp in an image, it will be exposed once until it is correctly exposed, at which point, as the exposure progresses it will be ignored. However, if another street lamp comes on in another area of the image, that will be added to the image which will now show both lights. And so on. The classic use of this would be a firework display. No matter how many fireworks go off they will only be added to the image if they make the area of the screen where they appear brighter than previously. Gradually you build up an image where the entire sky is a dazzling mass of exploding fireworks. The **Composite Setting** itself determines the base exposure of your image. If the fireworks are being set off behind a floodlit castle will need to set a proper exposure for the wall because that will be there all through the exposure and needs to be properly exposed for the picture to succeed. So if the camera is set to f/4 and the castle wall requires an exposure of 1 second at f/4, set the **Composite Setting** accordingly. Now, the castle wall will be exposed at the start of the exposure and will not change as the fireworks are gradually added (composited). The **Composite Exposure** forms the base exposure for your image, in other words.

Flicker Scan

 Under some kinds of artificial lighting you may see a banding/ flickering effect on screen. This will attempt to stop it. **Note:** it operates only on the **Silent Shutter** or the mechanical shutter in **S** or **M** modes.

Custom E3

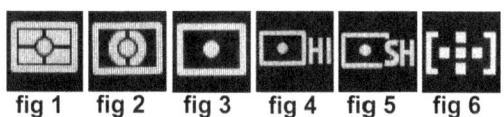

fig 1 fig 2 fig 3 fig 4 fig 5 fig 6

Metering

• (fig 1)This is called **Digital ESP Metering** It measures a matrix of over 300 samples of the scene brightness and calculates the optimum exposure. It's the best all round choice and often the only one you will use. If the scene looks to dark or light, a touch of **Exposure Compensation** will take care of it but it's usually not necessary. If you set Face Priority focusing, metering knows that and exposes with that in mind

• (fig 2)This meters the centre of the subject and the background separately and averages them. It assumes that the most important element of your picture is in the centre and weights the exposure to that. It's a method that was used by pre-digital cameras and is

superseded by the much more accurate and consistent matrix metering above
• (fig 3) Spot metering, this meters a tiny central point of the scene. The metering area is indicated by a thin circular overlay on the screen. It is of use where your subject is a small object set against a background of a radically different brightness. For example, if you photograph a crow standing in a snow covered field, the camera's exposure system cannot know that it is only the crow that you're concerned about photographing. It will try to average out the exposure, albeit intelligently, and the crow will almost certainly be under-exposed. Set Spot Metering and line the circle up with the bird and exposure will be made entirely for the bird. This is not perfect, however, because of the way that exposure metering works. It assumes that any subject will have an overall average

light reflectance of 18%. While that is true of many scenes, it is not true of a crow which, being jet black, probably reflects no more than 2% of the light that falls on it. The meter will therefore expose to make the crow look a mid grey - in other words over expose it! Spot metering is very useful on occasion but must be used intelligently

• (fig 4)**HI** light tells the meter that your subject is light and it exposes accordingly

• (fig 5)**SH**adow tells the meter that your subject is dark and so it exposes to preserve the dark nature of the subject. The crow would be an example.

Note: I don't use all these Metering settings much. Generally, I find it easier to use **Digital ESP Metering** and use **Exposure Compensation** to get the exposure how I want it.

AEL Metering

The **AEL** button is in the middle of the 2 way lever to the right of the EVF on the back of the camera. When you press it, it sets the exposure and locks it until pressed again. Set to **Auto** it uses the same metering method as you have already set. Set to any of the other settings, it uses those but does not alter the general method. So, if you set the camera to **Digital ESP Metering** and **AEL Metering** to **Spot**, if you are photographing a normal landscape and suddenly an interesting small bird appears, press the **AEL** button and you can meter just for the bird. Do remember to press the **AEL** button again afterwards, though. Otherwise you might end up setting the exposure for your landscape from the trunk of a single Silver Birch tree!

(fig 6)Spot Metering

Normally when you set **Spot Metering** (easiest done on the **SCP**) it will obtain its exposure reading from the small spot area in the centre of the screen. If you prefer, you can have the spot exposure reading taken from the **AF Target** area. The logic of this is that if you are setting focus to a particular area, that is where you would want exposure metered too. When you choose **Spot Metering**, you can set which types transfer their metering to the **AF Area**. Tick **HI** but not **SH** and **HI** will meter from the **AF Area** while **SH** will meter from the centre spot. **Note:** the centre spot still shows, even if metering is taking place from the **Focus Area**.

Custom F

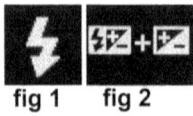

fig 1   fig 2

(fig 1)X-Sync

this sets the maximum shutter speed that can be used when the flash is fitted and turned on. The top speed is limited to 1/250th for technical reasons to do with the focal plane shutter that all Micro Four Thirds cameras use. You have options from I/60th to 1/250. If you have a moving subject with fairly bright ambient light and use a slower shutter speed you can get a double imaging effect due to the mixing of the flash and ambient light. When your main light source is the flash, therefore, it makes sense to use the highest 1/250th speed to eliminate as much as possible of the ambient light. A consequence of eliminating the ambient light is that while the foreground of your picture will be

properly exposed by the flash, the background, being further away from the light source, will be underexposed. Which is the reason that not only can you set the highest speed the camera will use but also the lowest - see **Slow Limit** below.
Note: the **X-Sync** setting applies to **P** and **A** modes. In **S** and **M** shooting will be at the shutter speed you set - but the camera will not let you set higher than 1/250th. In **Auto** all decisions are made by the camera.

(fig 1)Slow Limit

This sets the slowest shutter speed the camera will use when flash is being used. While **X-Sync**, the top limit, applies to all shooting modes, **Slow Limit** applies only to **P** and **A**. In **S** and **M** modes, you can set any shutter speed you wish regardless.
Note: Some examples are necessary here. I will assume that you have set **X-Sync** at 1/250th in all cases.

- You are taking party pictures at night indoors and just want well lit sharp pictures of your friends in front of the camera, dancing and fooling around. Use **A** or **P** mode and set a **Slow Limit** of 1/250th. Set the aperture to f/5.6. All your pictures will be taken at 1/250th at f5.6, in the dark room making the flash effectively the only light source. Your pictures will be sharp and well lit while the background will be dark, focusing attention on your subjects
- In the same scenario as above but while you still want your subjects sharp and clear, you'd like to be able to see some room atmosphere as well. Without flash, the room lighting would require an exposure of about 1/15th at f/4 which would render the dancing revelers very blurred. Use **A** mode. Set the aperture to f/4 and **Slow Limit** to 1/30th. You will have sharp and well lit friends but if they are

dancing there may be some double imaging/ blurring. This can be regarded as give some atmosphere to the shots if the blurring is not too great. It is an effect which can certainly be used creatively. You could set **Slow Limit** to 1/15th or even lower to use all the room's available lighting but then since you are hand holding the camera you'd run the risk of adding camera shake to the mix

• You are taking a portrait in a well lit office. The office has strip lighting which is very unflattering to your subject. You want your portrait to show the subject's working environment and so require a great depth of focus to get the both subject and background sharp. The light level of the room is 1/30th at f/2.8. Use **A** mode. Set the **Slow Limit** to 1 second. You will need to use a tripod for this shot. Set the aperture to f/11. The camera will set the shutter speed to about 1/2 second. Ask your subject to keep still! The camera fire the flash strongly enough to light the subject properly while adjusting the shutter to speed to suit the room light

Note: in the last two scenarios using long exposures you could equally well use **S** or **M** modes and set the slow shutter speed explicitly since those modes ignore the **Slow Limit** setting. The advantage of using **A** combined with **Slow Limit** is that you have control of the aperture and thus depth of field while the camera takes care of the shutter speed. If you set the shutter speed explicitly, the camera takes care of the aperture in a situation where the depth of field is your primary creative control.

(fig 3)

(Ambient light + Flash compensation) Normally **Exposure Compensation** applied affects only ambient light. So, if you were making a flash portrait at 1/60 second at f/4, balancing the room and flash lighting and you dialled in plus 1 **Exposure Compensation**, the flash exposure would remain the same but the ambient light would be upped one stop, lightening the background. With this set **On**, the room would still be lightened but the flash exposure on the face would be adjusted upwards at the same time. The time to use this would be if you were finding your overall scene brightness too low. **Note:** On the **SCP** there is a flash intensity control so I prefer to leave this item **Off** and manipulate my flash exposure, if necessary, independently of the background from there.

(fig 1)+WB

If you have manually set **W**hite **B**alance to (tungsten), if you take a flash shot it will come out with a bright blue cast. This setting avoids that by automatically setting the **WB** to **Auto** or **Flash** when the flash is activated. It doesn't alter the setting shown on the **SCP** while the flash is being used and it reverts to your own setting when the flash is deactivated. It is hard to think of a reason to turn this **Off** unless you want a colour cast for creative purposes.

Custom G

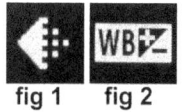
fig 1 fig 2

(fig 1)Set

This item determines the image quality choices you will be offered in the **SCP**, **Live Control** and **Shooting Menu 1.** The E-M5 Mark III offers a bewildering range of **JPG** image sizes from 20Mp to less than 1Mp with 4 compression levels rated **S**uper **F**ine, **F**ine, **N**ormal and **B**asic. With **RAW** and **RAW+JPG**, it comprises a list that would be impractical to traverse in a live shooting situation. For that reason when you want to change the image quality via the **SCP**, say, you are given a limited choice comprising **RAW** followed by 4 **JPG** flavours. (Those 4 **JPG** flavours are reflected in **RAW+JPG** too). **RAW** files are always recorded at the maximum pixel count, 5184x3888. Large files use the largest pixel count possible but the actual count will vary according to the **Aspect ratio**. Middle and Small can be tailored to your preference in the next menu item, **Pixel Count**. Image quality is a complex subject. When a file is compressed in **JPG** format it discards detail in order to lower the file size. SuperFine gives quality little different in practise from an uncompressed file but with large file sizes. **B**asic applies high compression for the smallest file size and in doing so discards considerable detail. It's horses for courses with **JPG** settings. For social media, Small and Basic are fine. If you want to make large prints, Large Fine or better still Super Fine are the way to go. **Note:** There are two ways of controlling file sizes. One is simply to make the file physically smaller, that is cut the number of pixels in it. If you have an uncompressed image 4000x3000px you have a roughly 34MB file. If you reduce it to 2000x1500px and you have 8.5MB file. Alternatively, you could apply a high degree of **JPG** compression to the 4000x3000 image and get the file size down to the same 8.5MB. There's no rule about what is best but high levels of **JPG** compression can lead to unpleasant halo and colour distortion artefacts on an image. So, if you know your image will only be seen on a 1920px width monitor, it is better to cut the pixel count to, say, 1920px across and compress less. Best advice is to shoot **RAW+JPG**. Then, if you want to post to social media immediately you could set the **JPG** to **S**mall/ **B**asic and post it without editing. Later in software export the **RAW** file to **JPG**s tailored to the medium which will display them. That way, whatever you do you will always have your original image to work from while maintaining the possibility of a quick upload to social media. Briefly, a **RAW** file comprises the unprocessed data stream from the sensor saved to the SD card. You will choose white balance, noise reduction,colour profile, contrast etc E-M5 Mark III for yourself in post processing, giving you maximum control over your final output in, usually, **JPG** form. An analogy with film would be that a **RAW** file is like negative. It contains all the information captured. A **JPG** is more like a print. It is the processed form of the information captured. Shooting just **JPG** is like making a print and then throwing away the negative. That's not a moral point - the JPG processing of Olympus cameras is second to none and for many photographers more than meets their needs.

Pixel Count

This allows you to tailor the pixel dimensions of **JPG** images shot in the **M**iddle and **S**mall **JPG** settings. If you display your images on a tablet, for example, **M**iddle at3200x2400 might be a convenient size. If you post to social media **S** at 1280x960 would be suitable. Given the capabilities of the E-M5 Mark III it would be a shame to shoot anything only at these sizes. That shot of your pooch juggling would gather a lot of Likes on Facebook at 1280x960 but it would be nice to have a full resolution shot as well when National Geographic want it for a cover.

Shading Comp.

All lenses give greater image brightness at the centre than at the corners to some extent. It tends to occur most in ultra-wide angle or ultra-high speed lenses and is most noticeable in images where there are large stretches of constant colour such as a clear blue sky. If you have a lens where you regard this vignetting effect as unacceptable, **Shading Comp** is the answer. Best left **Off** unless you need it since there is a processing overhead for each shot.

WB

This sets the **W**hite **B**alance. My experience is that **Auto** is rarely wrong. However, you can set **WB** explicitly to various scenarios from sunsets to underwater if you see on screen that **Auto** is giving unpleasant results. In the very unlikely event that you find any of the camera's default **WB** colour temperature options consistently 'wrong', you can adapt them individually to your taste here. There are 7 presets and 4 one touch settings. These are for use under conditions where **Auto** gets it wrong. If the appropriate preset doesn't look right, you can use one of the **One touch white balance** settings. To set one for your present location exit the menu and press **OK** to bring up the **SCP**. Select the **WB** panel and press **OK**. Press **INFO** and you will be instructed to point the camera at a sheet of white paper. Fill the frame with it (it doesn't matter if it is out of focus) and press the shutter. **WB** is now set for those conditions and can be recalled by using that preset. **Note: WB** is necessary because while the human eye adapts to the ambient light conditions without us perceiving it, the camera does not. A piece of white paper viewed in shade on a sunny day or in the open at sunset still looks white to the human eye. Actually, objectively measured, it is quite blue under the tree and quite red under sunset conditions and that is how the camera would portray it if left to its own devices. **WB** is how the camera keeps whites white when it records an image. If you are shooting **RAW**, you can adjust the **WB** however you wish in post processing, so in that case use **Auto** and change it later if necessary. White Balance is measured in degrees Kelvin, the lower the number the redder (warmer) the light, the higher the number the bluer (colder) the light. Candlelight is about the warmest light you'd normally encounter and is in the 1000k to 2000k range, a clear sunny day 5000 to 6500k and on a clear sunny day but in the shade 9000k to 10000k. A sunset might be around 3000k. What makes **WB** tricky is illustrated by the latter setting. If you set **WB** for the sunset to 3000k, a white will look white in your picture. But the reason we love a sunset is largely the sheer spectacular redness, the warmth of everything. We want it to be red. I say this not to confuse but to illustrate that white balance, like so much in photography, is not a matter of correct or incorrect but an artistic judgement.

All (fig 2)

In the unlikely event that you find the all camera's **WB** settings too warm or cold for your taste, this will shift the balance to your satisfaction. **Note:** it doesn't affect any Custom **WB** you have set. If you regret any changes you have made, **All Reset** will undo them.

WB Auto Keep Warm Color

If you are shooting under incandescent light, that is lights which work by heating a filament rather than low energy types, you may find the colours too warm. In which case, set this to **Off**. I prefer the warmer rendering of **On**. This does not affect results under other lighting conditions.

Color Space

This affects only **JPG** files. It does not affect the range or number of colours captured by the sensor.

sRGB is the accepted standard for almost every application and every display medium understands it.

• **Adobe RGB** is really a specialist professional standard which in theory has a wider colour range. However, used on normal display media, it leads to rather dull colours being displayed. It exists because in some professional fields they prefer to be given the wider range of colours so that they can tailor them to the colour space they prefer for their particular use or client preference. There is no gain and some disadvantage in using **Adobe RGB**

unless you have a specific reason to do so
- **sRGB** being the accepted standard for digital displays, outputting your images to that space gives you the best chance of viewers seeing your image as you intended

In the case of **RAW** files, you assign a **Color Space** of your choice when exporting to **JPG** so the setting here does not matter. **Note:** color space needs explaining. A camera sensor can capture far many more colours than any monitor or other viewing medium can display. However, in order to look convincing most images must have a range of colours spanning from black through to white. So we have a sensor capable of supplying, say, 20 million colours and a display medium capable of showing only 10 million of them. The output of the sensor must somehow be matched to the ability of the display medium. **Color Space** is how it is done. If you output to **Adobe RGB** you need to be sure that your image will be viewed on a display that understands and can use it. If it does not, the display will interpret the colours as best it can, the result often being a rather low contrast and lifeless image. In reality, the appearance of your image is always a hostage to fortune unless every step of the chain from your camera to every viewer's viewing device is calibrated.

Custom H1
File Name
• **Auto** As you take pictures, they are numbered so if you take 5 pictures they will go from 0001 to 0005. If you insert a new card the numbering will continue from 0006 and so on. When you import the camera files to your computer, there will be no filename clashes.

• **Reset** if you insert a new card, file names will start at the next number from the highest so like **Auto**, if you have 5 images, the next one will be 0006. The difference is that if you insert a new card, file names will recommence at 0001

Note: Unless you have a reason not to, **Auto** seems the sensible choice.

Edit Filename
This lets you edit the first characters of the filename assigned by the camera. You can choose the first 4 characters of the filename for **sRGB**

while for **Adobe RGB** a mandatory underscore is added and you can choose the next 3 characters. If you have two cameras you could identify which is which by this method.

dpi Settings

For screen and web viewing this has no effect. It affects only print quality. For example, the accepted commercial standard for high quality printing is 300dpi. If you make a 5188px wide image, dividing this by the **dpi Settings** will give you the largest print you can make retaining that level of quality. So, 5188 divided by 300 gives 17, meaning you can make a print of the very highest quality 17 inches across. A 50Mp **High Res** shot from the Olympus E-M5 Mark III would yield a highest quality print 27 inches across. In practice, 240 or 200 dpi is plenty for high quality prints so you can print even bigger if you wish. At that dpi the **Hi Res** image would yield a print 27 inches across. For news print, 150dpi is about right.

Copyright Settings

here you can set **Artist Name** and **Copyright Name** which will be written into the EXIF (Exchangeable Image File Format) if you wish. In these days of wholesale copyright infringement, at least the thief cannot plead that he didn't know the image was copyright - for what it's worth.

Lens Info Settings

Micro Four Thirds native lenses tell the E-M5 Mark III who they are via the array of electrical contacts at the camera/lens interface so that the camera can set the stabilization, focusing and myriad other settings for best performance with that lens. One of the wonders of the Micro Four Thirds system though is its ability to use old film lenses, cine lenses, cheap manual lenses, what have you. These lenses bring versatility to the system, filling in the gaps where native lenses cannot or do not go. I rarely use fisheye or very long lenses, for example but for the odd occasion I do, I have a cheap completely manual fisheye and a 300mm Nikkor f/4.5, which including the necessary adapter cost me less than £250. It would be very inconvenient if every time a non Micro Four Thirds lens was fitted, you had to go through the menu to select the best settings for it. **Info Settings** solves that problem. it lets you enter the necessary details once and from then on when you select the lens from the list those settings will be applied. To register a lens select **Create Lens Information**. With my Nikkor 300mm, I fill in Nikon 300mm/ 300/ f4.5 and press **Set**. Now, when that lens is fitted, I go to this menu item and select the correct lens from the list. If you have any doubt whether it matters, fit a legacy short focal length lens to the camera and tell it is a 300mm!

Custom H2

fig 1

Quick Erase

• **Off** When you press the (fig 1) **Delete** button while reviewing a recorded image in **Playback** you are asked for conformation that you want to delete it

• **On** When you press the button the image is deleted without further ado. Careful!

RAW+JPG Erase

If you shoot **RAW+JPG** and press the (fig 1) **Delete** button, do you want to delete just the **RAW** file, just the **JPG** or both at once. Choose here.

Priority Set

When the camera presents you with a **Yes/No** dialog, this sets whether **Yes** or **No** is highlighted by default.

Custom I

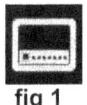
fig 1

EVF Auto Switch

With this set to **On**, the camera will sense when your eye is at the **EVF** and shut down the monitor and vice-versa. Some find the switching a little too sensitive (it switches over from monitor to **EVF** when your eye - or anything else - is about 5cm from the eyepiece. You can save battery power by leaving the **EVF Auto** Switch On and folding the monitor face in to the camera. Then, the **EVF** continues to switch off when you move your eye from the finder but cannot switch to the monitor since it is disabled face-in to the camera. **Note:** there is a power saving mode which does not involve turning the monitor into the body, **Quick Sleep Mode** in **Custom Menu→J2**

EVF Adjust

This enables you to tailor the **EVF** colour temperature and brightness to your preferences if you feel the need.

- **EVF Auto Luminance** With this **On** the camera adjusts the brightness automatically
- **EVF Adjust** When you select this, the monitor turns off and the brightness and colour temperature adjustments appear in the EVF itself so that you can judge the effect

Note: If you have **EVF Auto Luminance** set **On**, the camera is taking care of brightness and you can only adjust the colour temperature.

EVF Style

The main difference with these styles is whether the shooting information is shown overlaid on a full screen image or separately underneath a smaller image. If you prefer to see a clean image, even if a bit smaller, **Style1** and **Style2** are best. The only difference is that **Style1** has the information highlighted in blue, **Style 1** does not highlight it. **Style 3** fills the whole EVF screen area with the image and overlays the shooting information along the bottom and sides of the image area itself. **Note:** that if you like to use the **Level indicator**, **Style1** and **Style2** have the advantage that it can be displayed in the EVF when you half press the shutter (see **Half Way Level** further down this menu). It can't in **Style3**.

(fig 1)Info Settings

This affects EVF **Style1** and **Style2**. **Style3** always cycles between the 2 basic screens only. It controls what you see in the EVF when you press **INFO**. With all boxes unticked or only **Basic Information** ticked the **INFO** button cycles between two screens, one a clean view of the subject, the other overlaid with useful basic information like **Stabilization** and **AF** modes. If you tick **Custom1** it will add a third screen to the sequence with **Histogram**, **Highlight and Shadow** and **Level Gauge** shown if ticked. If you find that third screen too cluttered you can add a fourth screen to distribute **Histogram**, **Highlight and Shadow** and **Level Gauge** across two screens. **Note: Highlight and Shadow** in this context mean that clipped shadows, too dark for detail to be recorded are displayed in blue and clipped highlights, (too bright for detail to be recorded) are displayed in red.

EVF Grid Settings

This setting is greyed out in EVF **Style3**. Similarly, if you set **Custom Menu→D3→Grid Settings→Apply Settings To EVF** to **On** then this item will be greyed out since any type of grid you set to show on the monitor will automatically be shown in the EVF as well. If **Apply Settings To EVF** in **D3** is set **Off**, however, you can turn the grid on and off and control the **Grid Settings** for the EVF independently. The settings available here the same as those in **Custom Menu→D3→Grid Settings**.

(fig 1)Half Way Level

This does not operate in EVF **Style3** It causes the **Exposure Compensation** display at the bottom of the EVF to be replaced by a level gauge. It is different to the level gauge in the **INFO** display in that it only operates in the horizontal/landscape plane.

S-OVF

This effectively cripples your EVF in order to make it more like that of a DSLR, so that it will not show the effect of white balance, Art modes or exposure compensation, for example. It may give a better depiction of shadow detail, though it seems to be marginal to me.

Custom J1

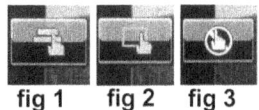

Pixel Mapping

This checks and if necessary corrects any anomalies in the camera's sensor and image processing functions. Unless you notice something amiss, there's not a lot of point in using this.

Press-And-Hold-Time

This sets how long you must hold a button down before it performs its function. The default on all buttons is 0.7 seconds, with a minimum of 0.5 seconds and up to 3 seconds settable. It is hard to see why you would want to slow down any of the button functions available. You could go through and set everything to 0.5 seconds but it doesn't make much difference in practice.

Level Adjust

If you find the **Level Gauge** is inaccurate, you can adjust it here. Make sure the camera is set absolutely level, select **Adjust** and press **OK**. If that looks worse, you can **Reset** it to its default.

Touchscreen Settings

Enable or disable the Touchscreen.
• **Off** Touch focusing and shutter operation will be disabled. When using the **SCP** you will only be able to select and alter parameters using the front and rear rear dials. Useful if you find your nose changes settings while you have your eye to the EVF

Note: when you have the touchscreen turned on with information showing (press the **INFO** button) you can control the touch operations with three icons on the left of the screen which you can cycle through with a tap of the finger. (fig 1), the camera will focus where you touch the screen and then fire the shutter. (fig 2), the camera will focus where you touch but you must release the shutter as normal. (fig 3), the touch screen is **Off**, overriding **Touchscreen Settings.**

Menu Recall
• **On** you are returned to the menu item you previously accessed

Fisheye Compensation
This only works with Olympus's own fisheye lens. You can get rid of the inherent (and desirable) barrel distortion of the fisheye, giving your picture the appearance of having been taken on a wide-angle lens. You can choose the crop type to best eliminate the blacked-out crop areas. You can even correct for distortion caused by under water use. **Note:** compensation is only applied to **JPG** files, even ig you are shooting **RAW+JPG**

Custom J2

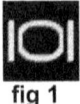
fig 1

Backlit LCD

The Monitor uses quite a lot of power via its backlight so it is wise to dim it when not in use. A touch on the shutter button, Menu button or the screen itself brings it back to life in an instant so 8 seconds is not too obstructive. **Hold** keeps it on

Sleep

this puts the camera into a deep energy saving mode after the time set here. It wakes up quickly, within a second or so, when the shutter button is touched.

Auto Power Off

If the camera goes into **Sleep** mode and is not woken up, after the time set here it automatically turns itself **Off**. If it does so, the **On/Off** lever will still be in the **On** position and will need to be switched to **Off** and then **On**

Quick Sleep Mode

This is a big power saver and really makes a difference. For this to work, the monitor must not be in use for live viewing. To achieve this, You can either fold it face in to the camera (the best way) or if it is facing out, press the (fig 1) **EVF/Monitor** manual switching button to the left of the EVF so that the **SCP** shows. The camera will now go to sleep as quickly as 3 seconds after being used. It can double the shooting capacity at the cost of instant readiness. If you are shooting instant street pictures, this won't work for you but out and about doing landscapes it is the difference between a days shooting on a battery or a half day.

Certification

This displays certification icons.
How did I ever manage without this?

Setup Menu

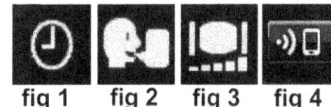

fig 1   fig 2   fig 3   fig 4

Card Setup

• **All Erase** This will simply erase all the images on your card. However, If you have protected any images they will not be erased

• **Format** This sets up an SD card ready for use in the camera. If you buy a new card, the first thing to do is to **Format** it in camera. Similarly, If a card is giving you problems of any kind, this is the first thing to try in order to remedy it. **Format** deletes all the images on the card - protected or not!

Note: images are protected in **Playback** grid view by touching the tab at the bottom of the screen where you will see a key symbol. Highlight the image you want to protect by scrolling through them with the front dial and touching the key icon. If you are viewing a single image, touching it will bring up the key icon at the bottom of the screen

(fig 1)

Sets the time, which us used ot time stamp your images

(fig 2)

this controls the language used for error messages, screen display, **SCP** and menus.

(fig 3)

If you find the monitor display too dark or light overall you can set it to your taste here. Ditto the colour temperature, basically the redness or blueness of the display. You can also set a more vivid display by pressing the **INFO** button. These do not affect the recorded image at all.

Rec View

After taking a picture the camera will display it for the number of seconds (up to 20) you set here before returning to shooting mode.

You are not stuck in **Rec View**, a touch on the shutter button returns the camera to shooting mode immediately. **Auto** puts the camera in Playback mode after the **Rec View** which could be handy of you want to delete it or do some editing immediately after capture. **Off** means the image isn't displayed after taking it. If you use it in **HDR** mode it displays the processed image for the set time once it has been processed. If you use it in **Sequential** it displays the last frame of the sequence.

Wi-Fi/ Bluetooth Settings

This is an invaluable facilitating remote shooting and location logging amongst many other things. The key is setting up the camera connection. Once done,everything else is easy and instinctive to do. Like all Wi-Fi and Bluetooth connections there is a little of the black arts to it so don't worry if you have to try a few times before succeeding.

1• Download the OI.Share app to your phone start it up.

2• Set **Availability** to **On**

3• On the monitor, touch (fig 4)

4• Press Next on th ensuing screens until you see 'Initiating', followed by a screen with a QR code displayed

5• On the OI Share app, touch **Remote Connect** and at the very bottom of the screen press **Easy Setup**. The **Camera Preparation** screen appears - press **Scan**

6• Frame the QR code on the camera monitor in the box that appears on the app

7• Press Start Setup

8• The camera will connect Bluetooth and Wi-Fi (this may take a minute or two)

9• On the app, press **Remote Control** or whatever action you require

Note: in step **8**, if the camera doesn't connect after a try or two, you can go to your phone and look through the available **Connection** list. You'll see the E-M5MarkIII listed there and a touch on that will make the connection straight away. Future connection will be a matter of simply switching on the Wi-Fi via the monitor icon

Availability

 This simply determines whether the Wi-Fi is **On** ready for connection via the monitor icon or not.

Connection Password

 You may need this if you make a direct connection to your phone, that is to say via your phone's Connection list rather than through OI Share app.

Power-off Standby

 With this **On** you can connect to the camera for the viewing and download of pictures without turning the camera itself on. The Wi-Fi will turn itself **Off** after 12 hours without use and also if you remove the battery or SD card.

Reset

This will set the Wi-Fi settings back to where they were when you bought the camera. Useful if you have problems setting up the Wi-Fi and want to start again. In such a case it can be useful to unpair the Bluetooth and Forget the Wi-Fi connection on your phone as well.

Firmware

This tells you the **Firmware** version you are using on your camera and lens. Olympus have a policy of constantly improving and upgrading their camera and lens performance by releasing updates. You can also update a Panasonic lens's firmware while it is mounted on an Olympus camera. Olympus recommend using their free to download 'Workspace' software for updates.

My Example Menu
Shooting Menu 1
- **Reset/Custom Modes - N/A**
- **Picture Mode** - Natural
- ◫ - LSF+RAW
- **Image Aspect - 4:3**
- **Digital Tele-converter - Off**
- ▭ - Single shot

Shooting Menu 2
- **Bracketing** - Off
- **HDR** - Off
- **Multiple Exposure - Off**
- **Keystone Comp. - Off**
- **Anti-Shock/Silent** - Anti-Shock 0/Silent 0/Off/NotAllow Not Allow not Allow
- **High Res Shot** - 2s/0s (using Micro Four Thirds compatible flash
- **RC Mode** - Off

Video Menu
- **(Mode Settings - S**
- **Specification Settings** - Mov FHD SF 30p/Standard/Off
- **AF/IS Settings** - C-AF/M-IS2

- **Button/Dial/Lever** - All at default/except Elec. Zoom Speed Low
- **Display Settings** - Live Control+Live SCP/Custom 1 ticked = Level Gauge/ Stabilizer/Histogram ISO/Time Code Settings N/A/Rec Run/Reset
- **Movie** - On
- **HDMI Output** Monitor Mode Off On -

Playback Menu

- - On
- **Edit** - N/A
- **Print Order** - N/A
- **Reset Protect** - N/A
- **Reset Share Order** - N/A
- **Device Connection** - N/A

Custom

A1
- **AF Mode** - S-AF
- **AEL/AFL** - Mode 1/Mode 2/Mode 1
- **AF Scanner** - Mode 3
- **C-AF Sensitivity** - +2
- **C-AF Center Start** - **All Ticked**

- **C-AF Center Priority - All Ticked**

A2
- **Mode Settings** - All Ticked (at first)
- **AF Area Pointer - On1**
- **AF Targeting Pad - On**
- **Set Home** - All Ticked/S-AF Single (not small)/Centred
- **Custom Settings (Set 1) - Mode/Face/Pos/Pos**

A3
- **AF Limiter - Off**
- **AF Illuminator - On**
- **(Face Priority - Off**
- **AF Focus Adj. - N/A**

A4
- **Preset MF Distance - N/A**
- **MF Assist** - On On
- **MF Clutch** - Operative
- **Focus Ring** - To Choice
- **Bulb/Time Focusing - Off**
- **Reset Lens - On**

B
- **Button Function** - All at defaults to start

- ▣ **Function** - Multiple Image Selection
- **Dial Function** - Defaults to start
- **Dial Direction** - To Choice
- **Fn Lever Function - Mode 1**
- **Fn Lever/Power Lever - Fn**
- **Elec. Zoom Speed** - Low (if fitted)

C1
- **S-AF Release Priority - Off**
- **C-AF Release Priority - On**
- **(L Settings** - 6fps Off/10fps Off/14 99
- **H Settings** - 10 Off/30fps Off/30fps 14 99
- **Flicker Reduction - Auto/Off**

C2
- ▣**Image Stabilizer - S-IS 1**
- ▣**Image Stabilizer** - fps Priority
- **Half Way Release With IS - On**
- **Lens I.S. Priority - Off**

D1
- **Control Settings** - All Ticked/Live SCP/All Ticked/All Ticked

- **Info Settings** - Image Only Overall/All Ticked/Image Only Custom 1 All Ticked/25 Calendar Ticked
- **Picture Mode Settings** - All Ticked to start
- ▬ **Settings** - All Ticked to start
- **Multi Function Settings** - All Ticked to start

D2
- **Live View Boost** - Off/On2/Off/Off
- **Art LV Mode** - Mode 1
- **LV Close Up Settings** - **Mode 2/Off**
- **Default Settings** - **X5**
- ◉**Settings** - Off/Off

D3
- **Grid Settings** - Preset 1/Off/On
- **Peaking Settings** - Red/normal/Off
- **Histogram Settings - 255 0**
- **Mode Guide - Off**
- **Selfie Assist - On**

D4
- 🔊 - On
- **HDMI** - As Required
- **USB Mode** - Auto

E1
- **Exposure Shift - All 0**
- **EV Step** - ½EV
- **ISO Step** - 1EV
- **ISO-Auto Set** - 6400 200/Auto
- **ISO-Auto** - All
- **Noise Filter - Low**
- **Noise Reduct. - Auto**

E2
- **Bulb/Time Timer** - As Required
- **Bulb/Time Monitor - 0**
- **Live Bulb - On**
- **Live Time - 4s**
- **Composite Settings - As Required**
- **Flicker Scan - Off**

E3
- **Metering** - Digital ESP
- **AEL Metering - Auto**
- **Spot Metering** - All Ticked

F
- **X-Sync** - 1/250
- **Slow Limit - 1/60**
- ▭ - Off
- **WB** - WBAuto

G

- ▣Set - As Required
- **Pixel Count** - 3200x2400/1280x960
- **Shading Comp. - Aoff**
- **WB** - Auto
- **All** - Defaults
- **WB Auto Keep Warm Color - On**
- **Color Space - sRGB**

H1

- **File Name** - Auto
- **Edit Filename** - As Required
- **dpi Settings - 300**
- **Copyright Settings - N/A**
- **Lens Info Settings - N/A**

H2

- **Quick Erase - Off**
- **RAW+JPG Erase - RAW+JPG**
- **Priority Set - Yes**

I

- **EVF Auto Switch - On**
- **EVF Adjust - On/0**
- **EVF Style** - Style 3
- **Info Settings** - Basic + Custom 1 Ticked/Custom 1 All Ticked

- **EVF Grid Settings** - On
- **Half Way Level** - On
- **S-OVF** - Off

J1
- **Pixel Mapping** - N/A
- **Press-And-Hold-Time** - All 0.7s
- **Level Adjust** - N/A
- **Touchscreen Settings** - On
- **Menu Recall** - On
- **Fisheye Compensation** - N/A

J2
- **Backlit LCD** - 30s
- **Sleep** - 1min
- **Auto Power Off** - 30min
- **Quick Sleep Mode** - As Required If On 3s 5s
- **Certification** - N/A
- **Card Setup** - N/A

Setup Menu
- **Card Setup** - N/A
- 🕐 - N/A
- 🌐 - Default
- 💻 - 0/0
- **Rec View** - 3s

- **Wi-Fi/Bluetooth Settings - N/A**
- **Firmware** - N/A

www.ingramcontent.com/pod-product-compliance
Lightning Source LLC
Chambersburg PA
CBHW071355210526
45465CB00001B/98